a9

Past Masters
General Editor   Keith Thomas

Homer

Jasper Griffin is Professor of Classical Literature at
Oxford University and a Fellow of Balliol College.

Past Masters

Forthcoming

Jasper Griffin

HOMER

Oxford   New York
OXFORD UNIVERSITY PRESS

Oxford University Press, Walton Street, Oxford OX2 6DP

Oxford New York
Athens Auckland Bangkok Bombay
Calcutta Cape Town Dar es Salaam Delhi
Florence Hong Kong Istanbul Karachi
Kuala Lumpur Madras Madrid Melbourne
Mexico City Nairobi Paris Singapore
Taipei Tokyo Toronto

and associated companies in
Berlin Ibadan

Oxford is a trade mark of Oxford University Press

First published 1980 as an Oxford University Press paperback
Reissued 1996

British Library Cataloguing in Publication Data
Data available

ISBN 0–19–287532–9

10 9 8 7 6

Printed in Great Britain
by Biddles Ltd.,
Guildford and King's Lynn

Preface

This book is not primarily about the historical background to the Homeric poems, nor their authorship, nor even their poetic quality, although something is said on these topics. It sets out to explain the thought which underlies the poems and is conveyed by them, with some indication of its significance for posterity and for us.

In writing such a book I am conscious of the debt which it owes to the work of many scholars and other writers, from antiquity to our own time; since detailed acknowledgement is impossible, I hope this general one will not seem a mere formality. The editor of the series, Mr Keith Thomas, and Dr Henry Hardy of the Oxford University Press, helped me to improve the book. My wife kindly read the proofs.

I have tried to give the references to passages in the poems which are important to my argument. In doing so, I have used Arabic numerals for books of the *Iliad*, Roman for books of the *Odyssey*; thus 7.64 means the sixty-fourth line of the seventh book of the *Iliad*, but vii.64 the corresponding line of the *Odyssey*.

Contents

1 The Homeric epic

> No exertion spent upon any of the great classics of the world, and attended with any amount of real result, is really thrown away. It is better to write one word upon the rock than a thousand on the water or the sand. (W. E. Gladstone, *Studies on Homer* 1.91)

Western literature begins with Homer. The two long heroic epics, *Iliad* and *Odyssey*, appear suddenly; we can know little about the poetry which preceded them, and composition in prose had not yet begun. They never lost their fascination for the ancient Greeks, and they continued to form the basis of Greek education, despite the passionate opposition of Plato. The Romans in turn fell under their spell, and Homer was the model of Virgil, who was to be the master and example of Dante and Milton; the Homeric poems are still the inspiration of Tennyson and Kazantzakis and James Joyce. If justification is needed for his inclusion in a series devoted not to literary criticism but to the great thinkers of the past, it can perhaps be found in the judgement of Matthew Arnold, that Homer is great 'in the noble and profound application of ideas to life' (*On Translating Homer*, 172). The aim of this book is to explain and justify that statement.

The first thing to say to all those who open a book like this one is that they should, of course, read the poems. No book about them can compete in interest or pleasure with the epics themselves. There are many readable translations, but none is completely satisfactory. Perhaps none can be, since there does not exist in English literature anything of the same nature as Homer, to serve as a model; as a sufficiently talented translator could, in principle, translate Sophocles into something like the style of Shakespeare, or Virgil into something like the style of Milton. The translations in this book represent an updating of the late Victorian versions of the *Iliad* by Lang, Leaf, and Myers (Macmillan, 1882), and of the *Odyssey* by Butcher and Lang (Macmillan, 1879), which aimed to turn Homer into prose which should be simple but also slightly archaic. But the enormous success of the Penguin translations by E. V. Rieu witnesses to Homer's power to fascinate, even in a colloquial guise.

Both the poems are about events in the story of the Trojan War. When Greeks became scholars and historians, centuries after Homer's time, they discussed the date of the fall of Troy; 1184 BC was the year most generally accepted. For the poet, the events of which he tells are set in a fairly distant past, when men were taller and stronger than they are now, and the gods moved among them. We are not told how long ago this period was, nor why there are no god-born heroes in the poet's own day. Other early poets did attempt to produce systematic explanations; that Homer does not is, therefore, a deliberate choice, and one which is in harmony with the tendency of his work to be interested in depicting events for themselves, in their greatness and starkness, not in attempts at rationalising and justifying them.

The Trojan War began because the Trojan prince Paris seduced and stole away the beautiful Helen, wife of the Achaean Menelaus, king of Sparta. It is an unromantic touch that he also stole 'much treasure' with her (13.626). Behind this story, but suppressed by Homer, lies the tale of the Judgement of Paris: called upon to decide which was most beautiful, Hera the queen of the gods, Athena the virgin warrior, or Aphrodite the goddess of love, he chose Aphrodite, who rewarded him with the most beautiful woman in the world. This was in its original nature a moral allegory: Which is the best and most desirable life for a man – to be a great king, or to be a mighty warrior, or to live in pleasure? And the point of the story was that the disastrous choice of Paris doomed his people. But something so flatly explicit and moral was alien to Homer's manner, and as we shall see he suppressed it, making the hatred of Hera and Athena for Troy something sinister and unexplained.

Menelaus' brother Agamemnon, king of Mycenae rich in

gold, was the greatest king in Greece. He raised a great expedition to cross the Aegean, punish the Trojans, and bring back Helen. The army consisted of many contingents, each with its own heroic leaders. The greatest warrior was Achilles, son of the sea-goddess Thetis by Peleus, a human father; Ajax, Odysseus, Diomede, and Nestor were among the Achaean heroes. When the *Iliad* begins, the Achaeans (also called Argives and Danaans) are at Troy, and we soon learn that they have been there for nine years.

The action of the *Iliad* begins with a quarrel between Agamemnon and Achilles over the distribution of booty. After a violent argument Achilles withdraws from the fighting to his tents, and calls on his mother to use her influence with Zeus to bring about an Achaean defeat, so that they will be forced to beg him to return to battle and save them. This plan gradually works, and in the ninth book Agamemnon, in despair, sends envoys with offers of gifts if Achilles will come back. It is made clear that by the normal heroic code Achilles should yield, but he so resents his treatment that passionate anger will not allow him to give way. So the war goes on without him, the Achaeans are harder and harder pressed, their champions are wounded, and finally with the help of Zeus Hector forces his way to the ships and tries to burn them (book fifteen). At this point the soft-hearted Patroclus, Achilles' dearest comrade, can no longer bear the disasters of his friends, and Achilles allows him to take the field, in his own armour, to help them. After great successes he is slain by Hector, who strips him of the armour of Achilles. Burning with grief and anger, Achilles resolves to kill Hector, although he has been told by his mother that after Hector's death his own will soon follow; he slaughters many Trojans and finally comes face to face with his enemy, who turns to flee but at last stands, fights, and is killed. Still isolated in grief and hatred, Achilles refuses to give up his body for burial and drags it behind his chariot. In the last book the gods intervene to make him surrender it: Priam is brought through the night to ransom the body of his son. The old king and the slayer of his son weep together, recognising each other's

greatness and the common unhappiness of men, and the poem
ends with the funeral of Hector and the lamentations over his
corpse.

The *Odyssey* begins ten years later and deals with the adventures of the last hero to return home from Troy. Between the
two poems the city has fallen at last, in the tenth year of the
war. Flashbacks give us glimpses of the Wooden Horse in
which the Achaeans made their way into the city, the burning
of Troy, the chaotic departure of the conquerors, drunken and
insolent, and the disasters which many of them had to suffer on
their journey home. Achilles was slain before the sack, Ajax
killed himself soon afterwards; above all King Agamemnon,
returning in triumph, was murdered by his unfaithful wife and
her ignoble lover. These linking passages between the two epics
are carefully arranged and put into the mouths of characters,
especially Nestor in book three and Menelaus in book four.

The poem itself concerns the return home to Ithaca of
Odysseus, most cunning and patient of heroes. At the beginning
he is lost to the world, far away on an island belonging to the
goddess Calypso, who loves him and will not let him go,
though he yearns for home. Meanwhile, his wife Penelope is the
object of the unwelcome courtship of the local princes, who are
carousing in his house and consuming his food and wine in a
campaign aimed at forcing her to marry one of them. His son
Telemachus, who was a baby when his father left, has hitherto
been a helpless spectator. The poem has a double plot, by contrast with the single plot of the *Iliad*: in the first four books the
goddess Athena rouses Telemachus to defy the suitors and go
off in quest of news of his father. He is entertained by Nestor
and by Menelaus, and we see him growing up in the course of
his travels. In the next four books Odysseus is released by
Calypso, under orders from Zeus; he builds a raft, sails away,
and is wrecked off the country of the Phaeacians, a semi-super-
natural people. From the ninth to the twelfth book he tells them
the long story of his wanderings and his encounters with such
perils as the Sirens and the Cyclops, and his journey to the
world of the dead. They then escort him home and leave him

on Ithaca. The two plots are united when Telemachus also returns home, avoiding an ambush by the suitors, and is united with his father. Disguised as a beggar, the hero is abused by the suitors in his own house. At length Penelope seems to give in. With many tears the great bow of Odysseus is produced, and the man who can string it and shoot through a row of axes is to have her hand. None of the suitors can bend the mighty bow; the hero gets it into his hands at last, performs the prescribed task, and then, with the aid of his son and two faithful retainers, destroys them all. After his reunion with Penelope the poem ends with a vain attempt by the suitors' kinsmen to avenge them, and Athena imposes peace on the island.

It must be said at the outset that of Homer as a man we know nothing at all, outside the poems which have come down to us under his name. When the Greeks became interested in biography, nothing was recorded about the man to whom they ascribed their greatest literary treasures. It is only a romantic story that he was a blind minstrel. The Greeks ascribed both epics to one man, only a few eccentrics attributing them to two different poets; but most scholars now believe that the *Iliad* was composed first, and that the *Odyssey* had a separate and rather later origin, the second poet being influenced by his knowledge of the *Iliad*. The arguments which support this conclusion are in part technical, being concerned with features of language, but some of them are more general and will be illustrated when this book turns to the *Odyssey*. The gods behave in a different way in the *Odyssey*, which also embodies another conception both of heroism and of morality, while the highly selective picture which the *Iliad* presents of the world gives place to a much more open and varied range of interests. It is not in the manner of the epic for the poet to speak of himself; the Muse inspires him and speaks through him, and in the twenty-seven thousand lines of the Homeric poems we are not told a single fact about the poet. The individual 'Homer' is lost in the splendour of the Homeric creation, and his name is in effect no more than a synonym for the epics themselves. Various considerations of language, archaeology, and history suggest that it was about 725 BC, somewhere on the coast of Asia Minor or on one of the Aegean islands, that a great poet conceived the plan of the *Iliad*, and perhaps a generation later that the second poet created the *Odyssey*, setting out to create a poem which in scale and inclusiveness should rival the *Iliad*.

Once in existence, the two poems never went out of fashion and were never lost sight of. It is the normal destiny of such early heroic poems, like the English *Beowulf* and the Icelandic *Edda*, to become old-fashioned, to be neglected, and, if they are lucky, to be eventually rediscovered. Sometimes, as in ancient Rome, by the time they are thought worth seeking they are already gone for ever. The Homeric poems never suffered this fate, but have been continuously read ever since their creation, first in Greece and then in Western Europe too. In this they differ from all the literature of the period except the Old Testament; the writings of the Egyptians, the Sumerians, the Babylonians, and all the rest were lost to the world for many centuries and have only recently been deciphered by the labours of Western scholars. Other reasons of history and geography kept our ancestors in ignorance of the literatures of India and China. They too could not directly influence European culture and history.

But although we cannot read the poems which went before Homer, it is important for the understanding of the Homeric achievement to have an idea of the background from which it emerges. This has several aspects. First, the Indo-European peoples from whom the Greeks are descended had a tradition of heroic verse. We find surviving representatives, for instance, in the ancient literature of India, in early Germanic lays, in the Anglo-Saxon *Beowulf*, and in old Irish. Such subjects as the anger and withdrawal of a hero, fights to the death between kinsmen or friends, feudal loyalty and disobedience, and perhaps above all revenge, recur in all of them; so does the conception of glory as the motive and reward of the warrior. We can see that Homer derives ultimately from such a tradition, and comparison with other branches of it can sometimes let us see the individuality of the Homeric poems. Revenge, for example, is a great motive in both epics, but when we look at the Germanic tradition, with the ecstasy of self-destructive violence to which the lust for revenge frequently impels heroes and heroines alike, we see a great contrast with the calculating rationality of Odysseus, and perhaps an even greater one with the deep self-knowledge and human sympathy which are shown when Priam meets his enemy Achilles in the last book of the *Iliad*.

In addition to this inherited tradition, early Greeks came into contact with civilisations of the East, already ancient and imposing. The stories of the Homeric poems are set, self-consciously, in the Bronze Age, when Mycenae was rich in gold; that means the period which we call Mycenaean, about 1400–1200 BC. The epics took their final form much later, but they embody real memories of that earlier period. It was one of cultural contact and even a degree of cultural uniformity over a wide area, from Greece across the Aegean Sea to the Hittites of Anatolia, Canaanite kingdoms like Ugarit in what is now Syria, Cyprus, Egypt, and even Mesopotamia. These kingdoms traded, corresponded, and were linked by dynastic marriages. More important, they produced literature, and we can see that Greece was influenced by it.

For example, Homer is familiar with the story that Zeus had a father called Cronos and a grandfather called Uranus, each of whom in turn was ousted from supreme godhead by his son. This succession of sky-gods makes no sense in terms of the original Indo-European conceptions, and it must have been learnt and borrowed from Eastern sources before 1000 BC. Again, in Homer we find repeatedly scenes in which the gods all meet for council and discuss human actions and destiny; this important feature, too, derives from the East, and we find such divine councils in the literature of Mesopotamia and Syria. They are alien to specifically Greek religion.

These two sets of traditions converge in the Homeric epic. We have also to consider real history. The poets retained an inherited memory that there had been a time when the king of Mycenae was a great ruler, the head of a host armed with bronze, in a Greece where the Dorian tribes, so powerful in their own time, had not yet arrived, the last of the migrant invaders from the North. We now know that real history underlay these ideas; Mycenae, in the classical period an unimportant place, was indeed a powerful stronghold in those days. But the singers, living themselves in the smaller-scale communities and poorer circumstances of Greece after the destruction of the Mycenaean palaces, no longer really understand what that earlier period was like or how it worked. The heroes and their world are presented as illiterate, while we know that the historic Mycenaeans kept elaborate bureaucratic records. The position of king Agamemnon is obscure: he is the supreme commander and in some sense 'more kingly' than the others, but they are generally represented as equals, free to accompany him or to leave the expedition, and when Achilles threatens to sail home from Troy Agamemnon can only say 'Run away, then, if that is your heart's desire; I do not ask you to stay for my sake – I have others who will honour me, and above all Zeus the Counsellor' (1.173). At moments we see a realistic picture of the circumstances of Homeric kings bearing more resemblance to those of farmers in the Dark Ages than of the powerful rulers who built the mighty fortresses of Mycenae and Tiryns, centuries before. Thus Priam's sons themselves harness his waggon, while he reviles them as wastrels and playboys (24.247–80); Priam himself feeds his own horses (5.271). In the *Odyssey* the arrival of two unexpected guests makes the servants wonder whether Menelaus' household will be able to cope (iv. 26–36). But at other times Homeric palaces are presented in terms which are imposing, if vague.

Above all, the age of Agamemnon is presented as a heroic age. It is not simply a period of past history which happens to be interesting. Men in those days were bigger and stronger than we are, and they were closer to the gods, who intervened directly in their actions and mingled with them on earth. Because the gods did this that time was a special time, and actions then had the quality of being representative of human life as a whole. We see and understand the nature and limits of human life as the gods intervene in it; the world becomes transparent, and we see the divine forces which act in the background and which in ordinary life are hidden. Many peoples have produced poetry about a heroic age, and it is implicit in the conception that what is aimed at is not a purely naturalistic or straightforwardly historical representation of a period of the past. It was because this period was felt to be special and to possess significance that stories about it are myths; the mythical age was quite short, only two or three generations about the time of the Theban and Trojan wars, and for the thousand years that antiquity lasted that period of the past was felt to be separate and continued to be the subject of poetry, tragedy, painting and sculpture. From Greece and Rome this passed to the art of Renaissance Europe, and it was as natural that the first operas to be produced in Italy should be on Greek mythical themes as it was for Shakespeare to write *Venus and Adonis*, Handel to write *Acis and Galatea*, and Leonardo, Titian and Poussin to represent mythological subjects.

It is one of the most characteristic features of Greek mythology that it is dominated by heroes and heroic stories. This makes it unique among the mythologies of the world. Normally we find far more about the gods, about the creation of the world, and about the fertility of plants, animals and men; and also about the activities of animals which can speak and have human or superhuman qualities. In most mythologies heroes are either inconspicuous or altogether absent. The paramount position of the Homeric poems in Greek literature is connected with this, although we are not in a position to find a simple relationship of cause and effect. The replacing of the colossal, the vague, and the bestial with the human image and the human scale is perhaps the most vital and the most lasting of all the achievements of Greece, both in literature and in art. In the *Iliad* that achievement appears already complete.

It was not achieved without self-conscious reflection and stylisation, and the careful combination of different elements. We see that the *Iliad* and *Odyssey* combine features from the Mycenaean past with others of the poets' own time. For example, the heroes are conscientiously represented as fighting with bronze, but incidental touches reveal that the poets were perfectly familiar with weapons of iron. They put side by side characters who look human and historical with others who had a quite different origin, like Helen, who was originally a goddess of vegetation, stolen away and brought back like Persephone the Corn Maiden, daughter of Demeter; and like Achilles, who is the leader of a completely mythical people, the Myrmidons, who is the son of a goddess of the sea, and who in most early Greek poetry (though not in Homer) was, like Siegfried, invulnerable save for one spot. The warriors at Troy are made to include the Lycians, living at the other end of Asia Minor, and Diomede, who belongs not in the Trojan cycle of myths but in that of Thebes; while in the *Odyssey* we find magical people like the Phaeacians and fairy-tale monsters like the Cyclops. In all this they are not unlike the German *Nibelungenlied*, which combines historical figures with mythical heroes and moves characters from century to century at will. These differences of origin are not apparent to the reader, because of the energy of the Homeric style and the consistency of the Homeric picture of the world. When they are pointed out by critics, they can help us to appreciate those qualities more fully.

The poems are composed in a complex metre. Like all Greek verse, it is built on patterns of long and short syllables; the stress accent which makes English poetry did not exist in early Greek. The unit is a long line, which remains constant in its basic pattern but admits controlled variation in such a way that it can contain from twelve to seventeen syllables. Both the length and the complexity of this line are unusual in heroic verse. The language is consciously poetic, and it contains words whose meaning was already obscure to the singers themselves, but which were felt to belong to the epic style. At the same time it can be very direct and simple, and it is not at all given to the rather humourless grandeur which is, perhaps, the characteristic vice of the style of such poets as Virgil, Milton, and Racine. Matthew Arnold, in his rewarding little book *On*

Translating Homer, gave as the chief qualities of the Homeric style: 'He is eminently rapid; he is eminently plain and direct ... and he is eminently noble.'

One striking feature of the poems calls for special comment, since although it is a matter of style it also has consequences of a more general sort. The Homeric poems differ from all other epic traditions, except those which derive from them, in their extended similes, comparisons which may be as long as a dozen lines. Sometimes a hero acts simply 'like a lion'; this may be developed until we read, for instance,

Achilles rushed to meet him like a lion, a ravaging lion, whom men are resolved to slay, the whole village uniting: at first he goes on, heedless, but when some fighting man wounds him with a spear, he gathers himself open-mouthed; there is foam about his teeth, his fighting spirit groans in his heart, and with his tail he lashes his flanks on either side, goading himself to fight, then comes straight on with glaring eyes, either to kill a man or be killed himself in the first onset: even so was Achilles driven on by his anger and his brave spirit to confront great-hearted Aeneas. (20.164–75).

Such a comparison becomes an end in itself, a striking piece of ornament and variety, and often it is unfolded in such a way that the simile differs from what it describes. Here, for instance, Achilles is not wounded, nor is he attacking a whole group of men. No doubt the avoidance of exact correspondence was deliberate; instead of the same picture twice repeated we see two different pictures.

Many of the similes are obviously heroic, derived from lions, wild boars, serpents, storms, floods, forest fires; others are drawn from trees, clouds, stars, the quiet sea. Many human activities appear, some of them decidedly practical. There are the agricultural tasks of irrigation, ploughing, reaping, threshing and treading out the corn; and such special trades as the smith cooling hot iron, woodcutters at work, the potter's wheel, tanners stretching out an ox-hide, a carpenter boring a beam, an artist gilding a statue, a woman weighing out wool. We see a little girl crying and pulling at her mother's skirt, women quarrelling in the street, a widow lamenting over her husband's body, a father recovering from an illness. There are 'un-dignified' similes, as when the slow retreat of Ajax, assailed by a host of Trojans, is compared to the slow exit of a donkey from a cornfield under the feeble blows of small boys, or Athena ward-ing off an arrow from Menelaus is compared to a mother brushing away a fly from a sleeping child, or Odysseus tossing and turning in impatient anger is compared to a blood-pudding seething over a fire (11.558, 4. 130, xx.25).

These similes add emphasis, and can direct the emotional response of the audience by presenting objects and scenes in a certain way, often in terms of exciting and dangerous things. But they also allow the poet to include aspects of the world which otherwise could not have been got in; wild nature, peaceful agriculture, the various trades and skills. Homer is confident that an enormous range of material can be described in the high style, without the risk of bathos or anti-climax; the whole world can be handled by the epic, not only battle and sudden death. This inclusiveness helps to create the conviction in the reader that justice is being done to reality, not just to specially selected areas of it, and that is important. It has been said that *Paradise Lost* could not include a child, because the naturalness of a child would be in too sharp a contrast with the formality of the poem's style; such a criticism could not be directed against Homer. In the later history of the influence of the Homeric poems, a fascinating study which cannot be tackled here, this is not the least important part of their legacy. Alexander Pope wrote that 'Nature and Homer were the same' (*Essay on Criticism*, 124), and the existence of the Homeric poems showed English poets that it was possible to be natural and also to be in the highest degree poetic.

In this century a great deal of work has been done on the theory, made famous by the American scholar Milman Parry (1902–35), that the Homeric epics are 'oral poetry'. Some features of the poems are very unlike written verse; this is obvi-ously true of the repeated and fixed adjectives which ac-company the name of each important hero and the mention of such recurrent things as spears or ships. 'Odysseus of the many schemes', 'swift-footed Achilles', 'Agamemnon lord of men', 'hollow ships', 'the loud-roaring sea'; they and their like present a notorious difficulty for the translator, since to omit them falsifies the poetry, but to render them every time seems to give them an emphasis in a modern language which in the original they do not possess. With these phrases go such constantly repeated lines as 'They stretched out their hands to the food lying ready', or 'Thus it seemed to him as he pondered to be the more rewarding course.' On a larger scale whole scenes, such as those of a warrior arming for battle, or a crew launching and rowing a ship, or the sacrifice of an animal, repeatedly appear unchanged, and when a messenger is sent with a communication he repeats it in the same words as we have heard it given to him.

After fifty years of scholarly effort it seems to be established that the poems are the end-product of an oral tradition, in which singers used these fixed formulaic devices to help them create, without the use of writing, long poems, which were worked over in the mind before the performance and recreated each time by a combination of memory, extemporising, and the deft use of existing blocks of words. It cannot be shown that our *Iliad* and *Odyssey* were themselves actually created in that way, and some scholars do not believe it, arguing that their exceptional length and polish are to be connected with the reintroduction of writing into Greece, about 730 BC, after centuries of illiteracy. The oral origin of the poems is not without importance, as it provides an explanation for features which strike a reader as unfamiliar; in addition, it should serve to warn us against building too much upon the repetition of a word, or a slight discrepancy between one scene and another. That is not to say that the poems need apology, and it is right to insist that they contain in reality very few significant discrepancies, and certainly none like the unexplained transfer of the title 'Nibelungs' from one set of people to their enemies in the *Nibelungenlied*, or the death of the princess Finnabair followed by her marriage to Cúchulainn in the Irish heroic cycle of the *Tain*.

After the final destruction in the twelfth century BC of the Mycenaean palaces and the developed culture which went with them, the end of a long process of decline, there followed a disturbed and much impoverished period, in which Greece was for a time cut off from the East. Old centres were abandoned, and artistic levels seem to have fallen sharply. The Homeric epics in their present form date from the end of this age, when Greece was growing richer again, and the alphabet was borrowed and adapted from the Phoenicians. Somewhere about 725 BC, it seems, the *Iliad* came into existence, at much the same time as other epic poems on mythological themes.

Although these other poems are lost, we know a certain amount about some of them, and it is clear that the *Iliad* is in important ways different. First, it is more than twice as long as any other we hear of, and very much longer than most. Second, it is organised in a different way. Whereas the *Thebaid* told the whole story of the Theban war, and such a poem as the *Sack of Troy* dealt with the obvious climax and end of the Trojan story, this enormous Troy-poem included neither the beginning of the war nor its end. It singled out an episode, in itself apparently indecisive, and made it represent the whole; the death of Hector means that Troy is doomed, while Achilles is also fated to die soon and has accepted his own death, but is still alive at the end of the poem. We shall see later how this is done. Third, the other early epics were very much freer in admitting the magical, the miraculous, and the bizarre. In those poems we find Amazons and Ethiops, marvellous armour which cannot be pierced, magical means which restore an old man to youth, and girls called Wine-girl, Corn-girl, and Oil-girl, who can produce without limit the provisions after which they are named. Among the Argonauts, Orpheus with his lute could control birds and animals, the two sons of the North Wind had wings, Lynceus had supernatural eyesight, and the ship itself could talk. There were magical objects. Troy could not fall as long as it kept the image of Athena called the Palladium; a hero suffered a wound which could be cured only by rust from the spear which made it; and so on. Above all, in those poems heroes could be raised from the dead, and we know that not only Achilles but also Penelope and Telemachus were made immortal.

Against this background the *Iliad* stands out as a conscious effort at something very different. We have seen that we know nothing of the author; we must add that we know as little of his audience. The *Iliad* takes a highly aristocratic view of human life, the common people being kept firmly in their place. That perhaps suggests an original audience which felt itself to be aristocratic in a sense in which that of the *Odyssey* did not; but such an inference is clearly flimsy. Whatever his hearers were, the poet had established an ascendancy over them which made it possible for him to impose upon them a very long poem, instead of complying with their more natural demand for something which could be heard complete in one or two sittings, like the songs which Demodocus sings in the *Odyssey*. Once he was embarked on something of the *Iliad*'s scale, the poet and not the audience was in control. We are to think of a singer, conscious of his own powers and the attention of his public, conceiving a massive poem, concerned with the subject-matter and drawing on the resources of the oral tradition. The poem was to be unified in a sophisticated way, including within the story of Achilles' wrath the whole of the Trojan War; at its end the audience were to accept that symbolically Troy had fallen. The whole conception, in scale and originality, was so bold and individual that we can be confident that it was that of one man. The days when romantic scholars believed in 'folk poetry', producing the *Iliad* by collective action, are over.

2 The Iliad

The *Iliad* begins by announcing its subject, 'the wrath of Achilles, son of Peleus, the accursed wrath that brought upon the Achaeans countless woes, and hurled down into Hades many mighty souls of heroes, making their bodies the prey of dogs and a feast for birds; and the will of Zeus was fulfilled'. The poet feels no need to explain who the characters are, or why the Achaeans are besieging Troy. His prologue takes for granted the whole story and tells the audience at what point the action is to begin. It also gives notice that the tale will be a grim one. This is not light-hearted entertainment, not the gratifying recital for Greek ears of the great victory of their ancestors over a foreign foe. Mighty heroes lying unburied, their bodies the prey of carrion beasts – that was the will of Zeus; we shall hear of terrible events, suffering for both sides, and beneath it all the dark purpose of the divine.

There were many stories of the anger and withdrawal of a hero. In the ninth book we are told another, that of Meleager, and there we learn that 'this is what we have heard of the fame of heroes of old, when violent anger came on one of them; they could be won with gifts and prevailed upon by speech' (9.524–6). We shall now see what the *Iliad* does with this traditional theme.

In the opening scenes of the poem we find the quarrel of Agamemnon, the leader of the expedition and the highest in rank, and Achilles, the mightiest warrior. They are introduced as 'Agamemnon, lord of men, and god-like Achilles', and the line deftly contrasts the man who depends on his rank and position, and the man who is marked as exceptional in his nature. The king has taken a captive girl as part of his booty; her father is a priest of the great god Apollo, and tries to ransom his daughter, offering rich gifts and hinting at the possible anger of the god; but Agamemnon harshly refuses. The priest prays to his god, who with his arrows brings a plague on the Achaean camp, forcing the chiefs, on the suggestion of Achilles, to consult the soothsayer Calchas about the cause. Angry and humiliated, Agamemnon demands to be recompensed for the loss of the girl and the loss of face; he utters a blustering threat to take a prize from one of the other chiefs, perhaps Achilles or another, and once that threat is uttered the response of Achilles forces him either to carry it out or to climb down in public.

The quarrel is marvellously described, each step following with perfectly convincing psychology, and at the end Achilles has withdrawn from the war to his tents with a great oath that 'the time will come when the need for Achilles will come on the Achaeans one and all, when in great numbers they fall dying at the hands of man-slaying Hector' (1.240). Agamemnon takes from him a girl captive whom he loves; Achilles appeals to his mother, the goddess Thetis, to prevail upon Zeus to get the Achaeans defeated, so that they will be forced to call on him. The next books show the beginning of the working-out of this plan. The Achaeans are listed, they take the field, the aggrieved husband Menelaus fights an inconclusive duel with Paris for Helen, and gradually the Achaeans are forced back.

The plot takes a new turn when Achilles, in the ninth book, finds that he cannot bring himself to accept the overtures of Agamemnon and to return to battle. In a passionate outburst of anger he says:

I hate his gifts, and I value him at a straw. Even if he gave me ten times and twenty times as much, all that he has and all that he could get, all the revenues of Orchomenus and Thebes . . . even if he gave me gifts in number like the sands of the sea or the dust of the earth, even so should Agamemnon not change my will, till he has paid me back all my bitter pain. (9.378)

He does recede from his intention to sail away home, but only to remain in resentful idleness while his friends continue to suffer. The intervention of Patroclus is needed to resolve the deadlock, and when Achilles allows him to fight in his stead, and he is killed by Hector, the theme of heroic anger and withdrawal is combined with that of revenge for a comrade, in a way which is truly tragic. Zeus has granted Achilles' prayer that his friends should suffer a defeat, but he asks bitterly, 'What pleasure have I in that, when my dear comrade is dead, Patroclus, whom I valued above all my comrades, as it were my own life? I have lost him . . .' (18.80). Overwhelming grief and remorse make the gifts of Agamemnon now valueless, and when they are punctiliously produced Achilles ignores them (19.147). He is no longer interested in the great quarrel with Agamemnon, and he lives only for revenge. So he returns to the fighting, transformed from the reasonable opponent of earlier days into a remorseless killer (21.100); only to find in the end that no revenge can be enough – not Hector's death, not even the dishonouring of his corpse.

Another motif, too, is brought in: the choice between a long life of inactivity and a short career of glory. Every hero, in whatever tradition, must make that choice. In its unsophisticated form it goes like the choice of the great hero Cúchulainn in the Ulster cycle. As a boy he learned that he who on a certain day took up arms for the first time would be a mighty warrior, his name would endure in Ireland, and stories about him would last for ever. He seized the opportunity. ' "Well," Cathbad said, "the day has this merit: he who arms for the first time today will achieve fame and greatness. But his life is short." "That is a fair bargain," Cúchulainn said. "If I achieve fame I am content, though I had only one day on earth".' But Achilles, brooding in his tent, can see no reason why he should make the heroic choice, since he has not been treated as a hero. 'I have spent sleepless nights and bloody days', he says, 'fighting with men who are defending their women-folk' (9.325), a picture of war which is chosen as unheroic, for the Achaeans, too, as he points out, are fighting over a woman – Helen. In the nineteenth book he speaks of his father, 'who no doubt at home is shedding great tears for the absence of his son, while in a foreign land I make war on the Trojans for the sake of hateful Helen' (19.322). And in the last book, brought face to face with the father of the enemy he has slain, he is reminded by Priam of his own father; both were happy once but are unhappy now. 'My father had only one son, doomed to an untimely death, and I am not even tending him as he grows old, since I have been sitting here in Troy, causing grief to you and your children' (24.540). The old motif has been given a more complex turn. Achilles does not become a pacifist; he has chosen heroism and he accepts his own imminent death, but instead of heroic satisfaction he feels a tragic sense of futility.

The story is also given a decisive extension in range and significance by the fact that Achilles is the son of a goddess and can mobilise the gods to intervene in his quarrel. Greek mythology knew of countless heroes who descended from unions between mortal women and gods. Originally this was part of the family pride of noble clans, whose claim to inborn superiority went back to a divine ancestor. Since Zeus was the highest god, most of these claims were naturally attached to him; hence his later reputation as a philanderer. But a union between a goddess and a mortal was a rarity. The gods tended not to like it, and it was felt that some special reason should exist for the man's good fortune. In the earliest stories Thetis was a mermaid and a shape-changer; Peleus wrestled with her on the seashore and held her fast as she turned herself into a lion, a serpent, a fire. At last he subdued her, but after bearing his son Achilles she left him and returned to the sea. Homer does not admit the weird aspects of this story. He lets Thetis say that she was married against her will to a mortal, but he gives no details; she is even spoken of at times as if she were a normal mother waiting at home, but we see that Peleus is in fact alone, and when Thetis comes to Achilles it is not from his home in Phthia but from the depths of the sea.

Thetis is humanised into a loving and suffering mother, but she remains a goddess. By involving Zeus in the quarrel of her son with Agamemnon, she gives it a cosmic significance: there are gods on both sides in the Trojan War. They are involved in the struggle hardly less passionately than men, and in their battles, dissensions and deceptions we see great human action receive added significance as it affects the rulers of heaven. All serious Greek poetry is concerned with the position of man in the world, and therefore with the gods who by their existence and nature define human life; this is as true of tragedy and lyric poetry as it is of the Homeric epic. The poet of the *Iliad* devised, in the figure of Thetis, a perfect link between the world of men and that of the gods. Not only does she have the function of setting the plot in motion; she is an intermediary between the human world of suffering and death and the divine world of contemplation and immortality.

Zeus, too, is used with great skill. The sky-father of popular belief, lord of the weather, the clouds, the lightning and the bright sky, to whom men prayed for rain, he is also fully personalised as a god who appears in stories, with personal relationships and all the difficulties that they must create for a supreme god. We see both aspects fused into one unforgettable moment when Thetis comes to him as he sits high and alone, and implores him to help her son, appealing to his memory of important services which she performed for him in the past. Zeus foresees trouble with his wife Hera, a vehement partisan of the Achaeans, if he agrees to injure them for Thetis' sake, and he sits in silence. She repeats her prayer, and at last he replies,

'In truth this is a sorry business; you will set me at enmity with Hera . . . But do you now be gone so that Hera may notice nothing, and all this shall be my concern. Come now, I will nod my head for you, so that you may feel confident. That from me is the supreme surety among the immortal gods; every word of mine is irrevocable and sure of fulfilment, if I nod my head in pledge.' So he spoke and nodded his dark brows; the eternal locks waved from the king's deathless head, and he shook mighty Olympus. (1.497–530)

The elemental god of sky and weather, sitting alone on the highest mountain and shaking it with a nod, is blended with the mythological god who has personal obligations to repay and a wife to be wary of. The combination is a strange and daring one, and it became the ancestor of many representations of the gods in action; not only the *Metamorphoses* of Ovid and their more or less frivolous descendants in literature and art (thousands of baroque ceilings with paintings of the gods derive ultimately from the *Iliad*), but also some of the puzzling aspects of a work like *Paradise Lost*, in which the Christian God and his Son must somehow combine transcendent supremacy with 'heroic' intervention in particular historic events. Homer has contrived to make his god, even amid these mythological embarrassments, remain sublime. The description of the nod, as compressed and weighty as his divine descriptions generally are, inspired the sculptor Phidias to create his celebrated statue of Zeus at Olympia, the greatest of all classical representations of the divine.

Homer's portrayal of the gods is a very remarkable one, which caused uneasiness and perplexity in later antiquity and which may disconcert the modern reader. Believer and atheist alike, we expect that gods will be shown as dignified, and that they will be primarily concerned with morality. Neither requirement seems to be fulfilled by the gods of the *Iliad*. Zeus does not, like Ares and Aphrodite, join in the battles of men and suffer wounds; he is not laughed at, like Hephaestus, nor does he have his ears boxed, like Artemis. At times, as we have seen, he can be sublime. But we must accept, hard as this is, that the dread Zeus alone on the mountain-top, whose nod shakes Olympus, is the same god as the henpecked head of a jovial society. The end of the first book of the *Iliad* shows how intimately the dignified and the undignified are mingled in the Homeric gods. Zeus, as we saw, sitting in majesty, replied to Thetis' prayer with anxiety about the trouble she will cause him with his wife, and the hope that she will not notice what is happening; an unimpressive response, until he adds the sublime nod of his deathless head. Zeus returns to the other gods, and they all rise to greet him, but the expected row with Hera breaks out at once. Zeus threatens her with violence: 'All the gods on Olympus will not keep me from you, when I lay my unconquerable hands on you.' The gods are cowed, and the lame craftsman god Hephaestus restores good humour, bustling about serving the nectar in the role which properly belonged to the glamorous Ganymede or Hebe. 'It is intolerable', he says, 'if you two are to quarrel like this over mortals; there will be no pleasure in the feast, for baser things are prevailing.'

This sequence of scenes shows how inextricably the sublime and the frivolous are mixed in the Homeric gods. The mixture is constant, and scenes in which gods are humiliated or ill-treated are regularly put next to scenes in which they reassert their glory. Aphrodite and Ares are wounded by the man Diomede in book five, and it is in that book that Apollo makes the most uncompromising statement of the unbridgeable gulf between gods and men; when Diomede tries to attack the mighty god, he thunders at him: 'Take thought, son of Tydeus, and fall back. Do not try to make your spirit equal to that of the gods; never is the race of immortal gods on a level with men who walk the earth.' Already we see the classic Greek injunction, 'Know yourself': not a recommendation of introspection, but a reminder of the chastening fact that you are not what you naturally aspire to be, a god. At the end of the book Ares is healed of his wound, bathed, and dressed in lovely garments, 'and by the side of Zeus he sat exulting in his splendour.' Even when Hera seduces and deceives Zeus himself, we find that the union of guileful goddess and gullible god is still the Sacred Marriage of Heaven and Earth which gives life to all nature:

The son of Cronos embraced his wife; beneath them the earth sent up new grown grass and dewy lotus and crocus and hyacinth, thick and soft, which raised them high from the earth. Thereon did they lie, and about them they cast a lovely golden cloud; from it fell shining dew. (14.346–51)

The gods are raised above men by their stature, their power, and their freedom from age and death. No longer do they fight serious wars among themselves, as they did once; no son of Zeus will fling him from Heaven as he flung his father. The divine energy of such gods might lack an outlet, were it not for the existence of men. In age-old religious belief, in Greece as in many other parts of the world, the sky-father was believed to look down from above and observe and punish the sins of men. Influence of the epics of Mesopotamia and Syria has led Homer to concentrate all his gods together in heaven; together they bend their eyes on mortal doings. This conception led to a new self-awareness both for gods and for men, who now define their own nature in the light of their visible opposite; it is only by contrast with men that the gods become aware of their own grandeur and unity. In addition, the gods, divided into parties by their passionate partisanship over Troy, become a permanent audience, and one which watches with the pure pleasure and pain not of a heavenly judge but of an audience at a sporting event, as when they all watch Hector pursued by Achilles round the walls of Troy, or at a tragedy, as when Zeus must watch his own son Sarpedon die.

The attention of the gods both glorifies human action, seen as worthy of such an audience, and also humbles it. We have seen Hephaestus protest at quarrels among the gods 'over mortals', complaining that the pleasure of the banquet is spoiled. Men are great enough for gods to care about their fate, but they are also so insignificant that gods do not take them altogether seriously. Zeus grieves when his son Sarpedon is slain and causes bloody rain to fall to mark his death, but he does not save him. The grief of a god for the passing of a mortal is of a different order from mortal grief. Sarpedon is not mentioned again in heaven, and the sorrow of Zeus is not like that of Priam for his son Hector, while of the gods it is only Thetis, who has entered into mortal life, who grieves as a mortal does. Gods may watch human struggles with passion, but at times they turn away; when Zeus has brought Hector and the Trojans to the Achaean ships, and the battle is raging, 'Zeus left them there to endure pain and suffering without pause. He turned away his shining eyes, gazing on the distant land of the horsemen of Thrace, the Mysians who fight close, and the haughty Hippemologians who live on milk, and the Abioi, most righteous of mankind; to Troy he did not turn his shining eyes at all . . .' (13.1–7). Such passages as this derive their power from the close juxtaposition of the two worlds. On earth, pain and suffering without pause; in heaven, the serenity of a god who can at will dismiss it from his thoughts, turning for variety to a long list of exotic and interesting peoples elsewhere.

Gods do all things with ease. The Achaeans, in their period of defeat, laboriously construct a defensive wall to protect their camp, and in the twelfth book we see the bitter fighting that is needed before the Trojans can breach it. But at the high point of Trojan success, three books later, Apollo puts the Greeks to rout.

So long as Phoebus Apollo held the aegis unmoved in his hands, so long did the weapons of both sides strike home, and men fell; but when he looked in the face of the swift Achaean horsemen and brandished the aegis, and himself uttered a mighty shout, then he laid a spell on their hearts in their breasts, and they forgot their fierce valour. As when two beasts of prey drive in confusion a herd of cattle or a great flock of sheep, in the dark night, coming suddenly when the herdsman is not by, even so were the Achaeans scattered in panic ... (15.318–26)

As for the wall, 'He cast down the Achaean wall with great ease, as when a boy plays with the sand on the sea-shore, first making castles in his childish play, then again in his sport shattering them with hands and feet: even so did you, archer Apollo, shatter the long toil and labour of the Argives ...' (15.361–6). For them, long toil and labour; for the god, child's play.

This picture is true no less of the workings of what might be called history. At the beginning of the fourth book, the two sides are making a desperate attempt to end the war by a compromise. The gods look on, 'drinking to each other from golden goblets and gazing upon the city of Troy', and Zeus asks whether they are to allow peace to be made without Troy's destruction. The two implacable goddesses Hera and Athena show their opposition, and Zeus asks Hera with emotion,

Strange creature, how have Priam and Priam's sons done you such wrong that you are furiously resolved to sack the standing citadel of Troy? If you were to enter the walls of the city and eat them raw, Priam and his sons and the rest of the Trojans, then you would assuage your anger. Do as you will; let this not be a quarrel and strife between us hereafter. And another thing will I say to you; take it to heart: when I shall be minded to destroy a city of men whom you love, do not hinder my wrath, but let me be, as I have given way to you, consenting with reluctant heart. For of all the cities of men on earth beneath the sun and the starry heaven, holy Ilium has been honoured most highly in my heart ... (4.31–49)

Hera replies, 'Three cities there are that I love the best, Argos and Sparta and Mycenae of the broad streets; destroy them, whenever they grow hateful to your heart. I do not defend them nor begrudge them ...'

Such a scene is heavy with meaning. The great goddess need not even answer, when she is asked the reason for her hatred; and Zeus, who asks for a justification, goes on at once to say 'Do what you like', with the result that she arranges for the truce to be broken and the war to go on. Zeus loves Troy, and Hera loves her cities in Greece, but when the *Iliad* was composed all four of them had been sacked, Argos and Sparta and Mycenae of the broad streets by the invaders who put an end to Mycenaean civilisation. When the audience asked for a reason for the destruction of the great cities of Greece, they were given this stark and terrible answer – a grim bargain among the gods, which made their patron goddess withdraw her protection. By contrast, when the Sumerian city of Ur fell to the Elamites, long poems of lamentation were composed which showed the goddess Ningal lamenting for her city and reproaching the other gods, whom she had vainly begged to spare it. That, I think, was the natural way for worshippers to imagine the god of a defeated people; again we find in the *Iliad* something much less obvious.

The hostility of Hera and Athena to Troy, which is shown as passionate and implacable, was connected originally with the story of the Judgement of Paris. As we have seen, Homer has suppressed the story, which was too abstract for his manner, but retained the hostility of the two goddesses, which becomes unmotivated and mysterious. As the gods need not be dignified unless they choose, so too they need give no reason for their attitudes and actions; again we are brought up against the hard fact of the supremacy of heaven, which places human life and suffering in the perspective in which the poet wishes us to see them.

We have seen that the *Iliad* creates a great Troy-poem about an episode in the war which appears to be, in itself, indecisive. The poet makes it clear that the death of Hector means the fall of Troy: he alone defended the city, we hear in book six, and when he was dead and dragged in the dust, his mother shrieked and tore her hair, 'his father moaned piteously, and about them the people were in lamentation and moaning all through the town. It was just as if all lofty Troy were burning utterly in fire' (22.405–11). We see the same technique of symbolic representation when the poet describes Hector's wife learning of his death when she sees Achilles dragging his corpse. She has been busy at her household work, weaving at the loom while the maid-servants prepared a hot bath for Hector on his return from battle. 'Fond woman, she did not know that Athena of the flashing eyes had slain him, far from any bath, by the hand of Achilles' (22.445–7). Hearing the lamentation of the Trojans on the wall, she rushes up and sees the swift horses dragging his body mercilessly to Achilles' ships. 'Dark night shrouded her eyes, then she fell back and her spirit left her. Far from her head she cast her bright head-dress, and the veil which golden Aphrodite had given her on the day when Hector of the shining helmet took her as his bride from her father's house . . .' (22.466 ff.). Just as the weaving and the bath are not simply random bits of fact but show us Andromache as the devoted and loving wife, so the fall of her wedding head-dress stands for the loss of her marriage and her husband.

We find powerful and important instances of this device elsewhere. One of the great skills of the *Iliad* is its art of contrasts. The virtuous Hector, good husband and father and champion of Troy, is contrasted with his glamorous and irresponsible brother Paris, childless seducer of a foreign woman, who is slack in battle and will be the ruin of his people. He is contrasted again with Achilles: the man with all human ties, a brave but human warrior fighting because he must, with the passionate and isolated half-divine hero, who does not know if his son, being reared on a distant island, is alive or dead (19.327), and who fights because he is a hero, aided by the gods and filled, after Patroclus' death, with superhuman power and ferocity. Achilles is contrasted again with the king Agamemnon, who is inferior in prowess, passing from bullying over-confidence to abject collapse and defeatism, and insisting on his rank to hide an inner uncertainty. The Achaeans as a whole are contrasted with the Trojans. Trojans show a tendency to be boasters, some of them are flashily dressed, they are more noisy and less disciplined in battle, provoking duels which Achaeans win. When both sides take the field for battle, 'The Trojans came on with clamour and uproar, like birds – as when the clamour of cranes rises to heaven ... But on the other side the Achaeans came on in silence, breathing resolution, with hearts resolved to assist each other' (3.2–9). But Hector, Andromache and Priam possess tragic stature, and the Trojans are never contemptible. And it is important that the distinction is not a mere reflection of Greek patriotism; the Trojans are shown as possessing the character which we see in Paris – the frivolity which led them to start the war, and which will naturally lead to their defeat. The story makes coherent sense; it is in fact moral, although the poet prefers to allow that to remain implicit rather than to spell it out, just as it is after all right that Troy should fall, since the Trojans started it all. In its broadest outline, whatever the behaviour of the gods as individuals, the plot of the *Iliad* does show the pattern of events as just.

These contrasts are brought out in scenes which have a representative value. The *Iliad*, as we have seen, does not begin until the ninth year of the Trojan War, but the indirect method of the poet allows him to include a scene which represents its beginning. The two armies are listed in lengthy catalogues in book two, and at last the Achaeans march off against Troy, their bronze armour glittering like a forest fire, the earth groaning beneath their tread (2.455–66). Word is brought to Priam, in council, of their coming: 'Old king, still you love discussion without end, as in the old days of peace, but now war without respite is upon us. Indeed I have entered many a time into battles of fighting men, but never have I seen so fine an army and so great . . .' (2.796–9). The Trojan host advances to meet them, noisy where the Achaeans are silent, and at once 'Paris, beautiful as a god, came out as champion of the Trojans, wearing on his shoulders a leopard-skin and curved bow and sword. Brandishing two spears he challenged all the chieftains of the Argives to fight him man to man in deadly duel' (3.16–20). The challenge is at once accepted by Helen's husband Menelaus, but 'when Paris, beautiful as a god, saw him appear in the front rank, his heart was dashed, and back among his friends he shrank in fear of death.' He has to be forced by Hector to put on armour and face the man he has wronged, he loses the duel and is rescued by Aphrodite and carried off home, where the goddess obliges Helen, now reluctant and ashamed, to go to bed with him. So Paris lies in bed with Helen, while out on the battlefield Menelaus hunts for him like a beast of prey: 'Nobody of the Trojans or their allies could point him out; they were not concealing him through affection, for they all hated him like black death' (3.448–54).

It is clear, first, that all this really belongs at the beginning of the war. This is, in some sense, the first onset of the Achaean army against Troy, of which Priam must be apprised, and in which the two rivals fight for Helen. That is made even more evident when Priam goes up on the wall with Helen and asks her to identify for him the Achaean leaders in the plain below; this, too, is strange after nine years of warfare. We see also what sort of man Paris is: his glamorous appearance in leopard skin instead of armour goes with his frivolous combination of light-hearted challenge and panic-stricken collapse. He is beautiful, but not a real fighter. And Helen, who now regrets her liaison with him, finds that she cannot get out of it; like the Trojans, who hate him like black death, and who will soon be fighting for him while he lies in bed with his stolen wife, she is now doomed to stay with him. This sequence of scenes, which the poet has by sleight of hand made to seem, as we read, perfectly natural in its present position, enables him to show us the nature of the characters and the significance of their actions.

Another such sequence is to be found in book six. In book five the Achaean hero Diomede achieved great things and even fought with gods; the main line of the plot, the Achaean defeat, seems almost lost to view. Hector goes off to Troy to tell the women to pray to the gods for aid, and above all to Athena. Again there is an oddity, on the level of common sense: if someone had to leave the fighting, why should it be the Trojans' greatest warrior? But the poet asks us to accept this, for the sake of the poetic benefits it makes possible. Hector comes into Troy and meets in succession three women. First, his mother Hecuba, a true mother, asks him to delay while she brings him a cup of wine, 'which puts great strength into a tired man'. Hector refuses: 'Do not bring me sweet wine, mother, lest you unstring me, and I forget my fighting spirit.' He then goes to Paris' house, to call him back to battle. He finds him in his bedroom, stroking his armour, with Helen and the maid-servants, a perfect tableau of the women's warrior. Paris agrees to come back, and Helen makes a moving speech, wishing that she had died at birth, or that she had married a man with self-respect and feeling for public opinion – a man like Hector, we are meant to infer, not like Paris. 'Come, sit down on this chair,' she says to Hector; 'you have the greatest share of the toil caused by me, bitch that I am, and the folly of Paris.' Again Hector resists the temptation of her charming company, saying that he must get back to the battlefield. But first he will visit his wife and his baby son.

Andromache is not sitting at home but is out on the walls with her child, to watch the battle. She pleads with him: 'Your reckless courage will be your death, and you are all I have ... Take pity on me and stay here on the wall, lest you make your son an orphan and your wife a widow. This is where the wall could most easily be stormed ...'. We see that book six repeats the same pattern three times, in a crescendo of emotional power: the woman attempts to hold back the fighting man, to keep him in her own world of comfort and safety. The temptation grows stronger each time. To Andromache Hector makes his most emotional reply, saying that he knows that Troy is doomed, and prays only that he may be dead before he hears her shriek as she is dragged away from the sack of the city into captivity and slavery. Over the head of the baby the wife smiles through her tears, and the husband, giving such comfort as soldiers do try to give their wives, goes back to battle. Not only do we see the fundamental contrast of the two sexes in their different worlds and different virtues; we also see the true marriage of Hector and Andromache contrasted with the guilty liaison of Paris and Helen, childless, a mere union of pleasure, in which Helen despises her man and tells him to go and fight and die. What a woman wants in a man is the resolution to resist her and to go out among the flying spears; but the frivolous Paris has doomed Andromache and her child. The series of scenes is so devised as to bring out the significance of the events.

We have mentioned the different virtues of the two sexes, and we might add that different qualities were also looked for and admired in young and old men: a young man was expected to be impetuous and fiery, an old man to be prudent and far-seeing. It is common in early societies to think of the excellence of a woman as lying in such qualities as chastity, beauty, and economy, while that of a man consists of courage, strength, and self-reliance. Thus, when Agamemnon is told that he must give up his captive Chryseis, in an explosion of unguarded rage he tells the assembled Achaeans that 'I value her above Clytemnestra my wedded wife, since she is not inferior to her in beauty or stature, nor in sense or handiwork' (1.113–15). By 'sense' he means the circumspect behaviour which enabled Penelope, for instance, to hold off the suitors. An ancient commentator observes that 'in one line he has included the whole excellence of a woman' (Greeks admired tall women, it may be observed). One might object that this list defines the excellence of a woman in terms of her value to a man; but it is fair to point out that the overriding emphasis on courage and strength as the virtues of a man largely defines him, too, in terms of his value to his women-folk. Human groups in that early world are constantly vulnerable to attack, and their existence depends on the fighting spirit of their men. Without Hector, Andromache will be a slave.

It is no less interesting that the qualities most highly prized are by no means exclusively moral. It will be centuries before Greece reaches the point where the ugly Socrates, condemned to death by his fellow citizens, can be presented as a paragon of moral excellence, or Plato can assert that really the nature and virtues of men and women are the same; and even with the immense prestige of Plato and the philosophers behind them, those views never wholly convinced the common man of antiquity. Perhaps even now, despite the long insistence by churches and philosophers that there is one single set of standards, unambiguously moral and the same for everybody, the common man still retains at heart some Homeric values. But while the standards of Homer's people can be seen to rest upon self-interest, it would be wrong to deny that they are moral at all. Loyalty, devotion, and self-sacrifice are central ideas for heroes and heroines alike. A wife can claim loyalty from her husband – 'every good and sensible man loves and cares for his wife', says Achilles (9.341), while Odysseus' father paid a high price for the maid-servant Eurycleia 'and honoured her as highly as his wife; but he never laid a hand on her, avoiding his wife's anger' (i.430–3) – as a soldier has a right to claim it from a comrade (9.628–45). The hero is subject to moral constraints.

The *Iliad* is a heroic poem, and it confronts the audience with the same central question which confronts the characters themselves: what is it to be a hero? It is on this that the energies of the poem are concentrated. To make this clear, it is rewarding to consider the question of Homeric realism. We find that the *Iliad* offers a highly stylised picture of human life and of the world, which none the less satisfies the reader that it is realistic, both in the sense of carrying conviction from moment to moment of the action, and also in the deeper sense of doing justice to the central facts of human life.

In the narrative of the poem there is no weather, in the ordinary sense. There is thunder, but only as a mark of the disastrous plans of Zeus and as an indication of future suffering; when a son of Zeus is slain in the fighting, his father sends bloody rain to distinguish his death; when the fighting grows exceptionally grim and slaughterous, dark clouds cover the combatants. In all this we see that the weather exists only as a reflection and intensification of events on the battlefield. We are not even told what is the season of the year during the unfolding of the action. Similarly, the topography of the scene of battle is shifting and inconstant. In the early part of the poem the rivers which cross the plain are apparently small and present no great obstacle to the warriors, but in books twenty and twenty-one the River Scamander becomes a formidable menace; this is in preparation for the extraordinary events of the latter part of twenty-one, in which Achilles actually fights the river. In book twenty-two we find, to our surprise, that the Scamander has two springs on the Trojan plain, one of hot and one of cold water. No search has ever found a hot spring in the area, and in another place it is said, much more plausibly, that the river rose on the slopes of Mount Ida (22.147, 12.21). Trees and rocks appear as they are needed for the action, and when not needed they are not present.

It is perhaps to be expected that in a heroic epic the ignoble bodily functions are ignored, although some heroic traditions, like the Irish, are less reticent in this respect. It is much more remarkable that fighting, too, is highly stylised. The whole emphasis is on the heroic duel, and many hundreds of lines consist of inimitably dispassionate descriptions of the slaying of heroes in single combat. A hero does not die of a chance wound, like King Ahab, slain by an arrow 'shot at a venture', or King Harold, hit in the eye by an archer. Nor do heroes suffer disabling wounds which fail to kill. When wounded, they either die at once or retire, to return later to battle. An Achaean hero is several times cut off by a number of Trojans and attacked by them all at once; no hero is killed in this way. The poem virtually excludes trickery and treason, too. From another side, we have already seen that magic weapons are excluded. What we are left with is the picture of the hero facing death at the hands of another hero. As the two come together, the rest of the world is tacitly abolished; the two men can challenge each other and converse as if they were anywhere but in the midst of furious fighting. The technique has much in common with that of the climax of a traditional Western film, and indeed it is there that we should look for the best modern parallel to the Homeric duel.

All attention is focused on the clash of heroes, and everything which could blur or detract from their encounter is as far as possible stylised away. All this is, in a sense, unrealistic, and that effect is intensified by the way in which the heroes are presented as superhuman. At the moment of rushing into such a clash the hero is raised to his highest power. All through the poem, heroes are compared to gods: 'the equal of Ares, god of war', 'a man equal to the gods', 'god-like', 'resembling the immortals' – no adjectives are more commonly applied to these warriors. As King Agamemnon marshals his great army he is said to be 'in eyes and head like Zeus who delights in thunder, in girdle like Ares, in chest like Poseidon' (2.478). King Priam of Troy says of his own son Hector that 'he was a god among men, and he seemed like the son not of a mortal man but of a god' (24.259).

While the hero lives, he is god-like and loved by the gods. In his martial rage, the high point and zenith of his existence, he is compared to a lion, a wild boar, a storm, a river in flood, a raging forest fire, a bright star from a dark cloud; his armour blazes like the sun, his eyes flash fire, his breast is filled with irresistible fury, his limbs are light and active. Encouraged by gods, he leaps at his enemy with a terrifying cry. When a hero is slain, the poet gives a detailed account of the moment of death. One is stabbed in the back as he flees, and lies in the dust, stretching out his hands to his friends; another dies bellowing with pain, clutching the bloody earth, or biting the cold bronze which has severed his tongue, or wounded between the navel and the genitals, 'where the wound is most painful for poor mortal men', writhing like a roped bull about the spear; or stabbed as he begs for his life, his liver thrust out with the spear and his lap filled with his blood. Hateful darkness seizes him, and his soul goes down to Hades bewailing its fate, leaving behind its youth and strength. After the horror of such a death nothing remains for the soul but a dark and comfortless world, the mouldering house of Hades, and a shadowy and senseless existence, forever banished from the light and warmth and activity of life. For the poet has abolished from the world any form of posthumous reward or blessedness, insisting that death is the end of everything sweet. It is also made very explicit that the dead are wholly cut off, that they have no power, and that they cannot intervene in the world of the living. This is contrary to the virtually unanimous view held in early societies, and in fact Homer's contemporaries did bring offerings to the tombs of the mighty dead, which of course implies their continuing power; Homer's conception is again his own.

We see how all this works together to concentrate on the contrast of life and death, and to make it as absolute as possible. Alive, the hero is full of vitality and power, splendid and terrible; every time he goes into battle he must accept the risk of death, in its full horror and finality. No hero, not even Achilles, is spared the humiliating experience of fear. It is this which makes us feel that despite the stylisation and the omissions (there are for instance no maimed but living casualties like those of the poetry of the First World War), Homer's treatment of war is nevertheless realistic. Whole books of the poem are dominated by the fact of death in its most concrete and most horrific form, the corpse of the warrior. The anger of Achilles, we are told at the beginning of the first book, 'sent down to Hades many mighty souls of heroes, and made them the prey of dogs and a feast for birds; and the will of Zeus was fulfilled.' The hero faces not simply death, but also the nightmare terror that after death his body will be mutilated by the enemy and devoured by carrion beasts. Over the bodies of Sarpedon and Patroclus rages the most bitter fighting of the whole of the *Iliad*, and the end of the poem is built round the corpse of Hector, dishonoured by Achilles but preserved by the gods and eventually restored to his father Priam. The very greatest heroes may be delivered after death by their friends or guarded by gods, but the poet tells us also of the undistinguished dead whose bodies are driven over by chariots, splashing the axles and wheels with their blood (20.499), and who at best are collected on carts early next morning:

Now the sun was newly striking the fields as he climbed the sky from the deep stream of quiet Ocean, when men from both sides met. Then it was hard to recognise each man, but they washed away the clotted blood with water, shedding hot tears, and lifted them on to waggons. Priam forbade them to weep aloud; in silence, grieving at heart, the Trojans heaped the corpses on the pyre and burned them, and then went back to the stronghold of Troy. And in the same manner the Achaeans on their side heaped their corpses on the pyre, grieving at heart . . . (7.421–31)

This terrible emphasis on death makes it clear that the *Iliad* is very far from being a naïve or sentimental glorification of war. Among the regular phrases which it applies to battle are both 'battle where men win glory' and also 'battle which brings tears'. Both aspects are equally real. We saw above both Agamemnon and Hector compared with gods, and we realise the complexity of that idea when we remember that at those very moments Agamemnon is being led by Zeus to disaster, while Hector is dead, his body in the power of his ruthless enemy. More poignantly still, when Sarpedon, son of Zeus, is dead, and his body is fought over by the two armies, 'then not even a discerning man would have recognised god-like Sarpedon, for he was covered with weapons and blood and dirt, from his head right down to his feet' (16.638). That is all that is left of the handsome warrior Sarpedon, who in life was like a god. For the poet, the greatness and the fragility of man go inseparably together, and it is their combination which makes up the nature of the hero. The existence of the gods, ageless and deathless, yet resembling men, enables the poet to bring out his conception of human nature with great vividness, by comparing and contrasting his heroes with his gods. A last example shows how this device makes possible effects of great economy and power. When Patroclus is called by Achilles to go on the mission which will lead to his return to battle and to his death, the poet presents him in one line: 'He came out, the equal of Ares; and that was the beginning of his doom' (11.604). We see him simultaneously as a man at the zenith of human splendour, and as a vulnerable creature marked out for death.

Men can resemble gods; gods can love men. Zeus himself loves Hector and Sarpedon, Patroclus and Achilles; he also loves Agamemnon. The kings who fight at Troy are descended from Zeus, according to their formulaic titles, and Zeus himself tells us that he loves Troy more than any city beneath the starry heaven (4.44). But at the end of the *Iliad* Sarpedon, Patroclus and Hector are all dead, Achilles is soon to die, and Troy is doomed; King Agamemnon has had to learn the bitter lesson that Zeus was prepared to deceive and humiliate him for Achilles' sake. Hera says of Peleus, the father of Achilles, that 'he was dearest of all men to the heart of the immortals, and all the gods were present at his wedding' (24.61), but now Peleus is old and pitiable, and his son says 'Yet even on him God has brought suffering. He has had no offspring of strong sons in his house, but one son doomed to an untimely death; and I am not caring for him as he grows old, but I sit in Troy, far from home, bringing grief on you and your children' (24.538).

As Hector is pursued by Achilles, all the gods look on, and Zeus says 'Alas, I see a man whom I love pursued round the wall, and my heart laments for Hector' (22.168). When his own son Sarpedon is dead and unrecognisable in blood and dirt, 'Zeus never turned his shining eyes away from the mighty battle' (16.645). After Hector's death, while Achilles is abusing his corpse and will not surrender it, his old father Priam lies grovelling among the cow-dung in the courtyard in the ecstasy of his grief; Zeus sends Iris, the divine messenger, to him to bid him go alone into Achilles' presence, and Iris says 'Zeus, far away, pities you and cares for you.' It is suffering which enables mortal men to establish a claim on the serious interest of the gods, and the divine gaze is fixed upon those who suffer most. It is because they are doomed that Zeus loves them, a conception which later became a cliché in the form 'those whom the gods love die young', but which in the *Iliad* is a genuinely tragic view of the world and human life. It is above all as the hero, in the brilliance of his heroism, approaches the sudden transition to death and darkness, that his being takes on a new and poignant vividness which attracts the divine eye. In that combination of light and shadow Zeus sees and loves him for what he is, his nature being at once at its most god-like and its most human. Most of the characters in the poem have little insight into this tragic background of events; both Hector and Patroclus are deceived by success and fail to recognise that their temporary victories are, in the plan of Zeus, only a stage in their intended defeat and death. It is only a few who see further and understand more.

Helen, about whom the fighting rages, has achieved a true perspective. The poet shows us that she thinks of herself as a character in history, someone who will be remembered for her role in terrible events. When Menelaus and Paris are to fight for her hand, Iris comes to take her up on to the wall to watch the duel (and, we add, to be visible as the prize). Iris finds Helen 'weaving at the great loom a double crimson cloth, and embroidering in it many battles of the horse-taming Trojans and the Achaeans in brazen armour, all that they were suffering in war for her sake' (3.125). This symbolic scene is made explicit later, when she asks Hector to sit beside her, 'since you have most trouble at heart because of me, bitch that I am, and the sin of Paris. Zeus has imposed an evil fate upon us, so that hereafter we may be sung of by men to come' (6.355). In the *Odyssey* Helen is presented in very much the same way. When young Telemachus, Odysseus' son, leaves her house in Sparta, he is of course given a present by Menelaus. Helen, then, unexpectedly, gives him a present of her own, a woman's dress which she has made herself: 'I too give you a present, a keepsake of the hands of Helen, for your bride to wear on the joyous day of your wedding' (xv.125). She knows that the dress will have special value because of its maker, and she refers to herself by name, like a figure in history; any bride will be flattered to wear what the legendary Helen made. And Helen is a legendary

figure not for her achievements or her virtue but for her guilt
and suffering. Similarly, in other passages of the *Odyssey*, King
Alcinous tells Odysseus that 'the gods planned the doom of the
Argives and of Troy, and they wove the threads of destruction
for men, so that there should be a song for men to come'
(viii.578), and Telemachus tells his mother Penelope to listen in
patience to the song of the disastrous return of the Achaeans
from Troy, and to realise that many others besides herself have
had suffering decreed for them by Zeus (i.353).

It is suffering which produces song, and by song we understand that suffering is the universal lot of man. It is part of the
greatness of Achilles that he sees this with a clarity beyond the
reach of Agamemnon or Hector. When Hector has given Patroclus his fatal wound, the dying hero prophesies the imminent
death of his slayer at the hands of Achilles. Hector replies,
'Patroclus, why do you predict sheer death for me? Who knows
if Achilles, the son of fair-haired Thetis, may not first be smit-
ten by my spear and lose his life?' (16.859). In a deliberate contrast, when the dying Hector warns Achilles of his imminent
death at the hands of Paris and Phoebus Apollo, Achilles
replies, 'Die! as for my death, I will accept it whenever Zeus
wills it with the other immortal gods' (22.365). Achilles accepts
his own death, which his goddess mother has told him is near at
hand. His acceptance ennobles and makes bearable his terrific
outburst of slaughter in books twenty to twenty-two, as we see
in the encounter with the Trojan prince Lycaon. This un-
fortunate son of Priam had been captured by Achilles and sold
into slavery. He is ransomed by his friends, and on the twelfth
day after his return Achilles comes upon him again, unarmed,
cooling off after running away. Lycaon begs for his life, holding Achilles' spear, but the hero's reply is terrible.

'Come, my friend, die in your turn; why lament like this? Patroclus
is dead, who was a much better man than you. Do you not see what a
man I am in stature and beauty? My father is a hero, my mother a
goddess – yet even upon me wait death and mighty fate. There will
be a morning or an evening or a midday when a man will take my
life, either with a spear or an arrow from the bow.' So he spoke, and

the courage and strength of Lycaon failed him; he let go of the spear and sat with arms outspread. But Achilles drew his sharp sword and struck him on the collar-bone by the neck, and all the two-edged blade entered into him ... (21.106–19)

Achilles, who is capable of this vision of life and death, grim but unsentimental, and expressed in a tone almost intimate, speaks also of the obligations of heroism with the same disillusioned power (above, pages 18–19). The climax of it all, and perhaps the high point of the whole poem, is his encounter with Priam in the last book. The old king has come alone, by night, bringing the ransom for the body of his son Hector, into the enemy camp and into the presence of the man who killed his son. He kisses Achilles' hands and begs him to accept the ransom, reminding him of his own father, who also is old and helpless.

So Priam spoke, and awoke in Achilles the desire to weep for his father. He touched the old man's hand and gently pushed him away. And they both remembered their dead; Priam wept for man-slaying Hector, crouched at Achilles' feet, and Achilles wept for his own father, and also for Patroclus ... (24.507–11)

Then Achilles raises Priam to a chair and in a long speech expresses the deep humanism of the poet. All men must suffer; that is the way the gods plan human life, 'while they themselves are free from care'. Achilles' own father Peleus was loved by the gods, and now he is old and alone, 'while I sit far away, here in Troy, bringing grief on you and your children. You too, old man, we hear were happy once ...' (24.540). The epic might have ended with the slaying of Hector. The ending which the poet has devised allows his poem to finish, not with a mere heroic triumph, but with great opponents meeting at a level from which they see, with deep pathos but without bitterness or self-pity, the fundamental condition of the life of man. Achilles and Priam recognise their kinship in mortality and suffering; Achilles overrules the reluctance of Priam and obliges him to eat with him, a universal symbol of union, and then

When they had despatched desire for food and drink, then Priam son

of Dardanus marvelled at Achilles, his stature and his beauty, for he
was like a god to look upon. And Achilles marvelled at Priam, be-
holding his noble aspect and listening to his words. (24.628–32)

This very Greek sensitivity, even at such a moment, to beauty,
which is present not only in the young warrior but also in the
old king, gives the last touch to the scene. We see the poet give a
concrete example of his conception that it is out of suffering
and disaster that beauty emerges. Achilles and Priam are
brought together by the terrible fact that Achilles has killed
Hector, and the war will go on until Troy is destroyed; but
their encounter enables them to show a high civility, and to
recognise in each other both the splendour and the fragility
which are united in the nature of man.

From this conception there descended ideas which were to be of
great importance in the later history of Europe. First, the idea
that accepting destiny ennobles and transforms the mere
necessity of enduring it, the difference between Achilles, who
understands, and Agamemnon and Hector, who do not. The
Stoics, from 300 BC throughout later antiquity, taught the vital
importance of identifying one's own will with the will of God
as revealed in what happens to one: 'Fate leads you if you
assent, drags you if you do not' (Seneca), and that line of
thought was to live on as an important Christian doctrine. One
ought not to repine against the ways of Providence. Not only a
passive obedience, however, but also a consciously heroic attitude to the hard rule of fate can be learned from Homer. We
have a striking example of the inspiration of a truly aristocratic
spirit in a contemporary story of Lord Granville, President of
the Council in 1762, at work on the text of the Treaty of Paris.
Robert Wood, who brought him the draft a few days before
Granville's death, tells the story: 'I found him so languid that I
proposed postponing my business for another time; but he
insisted that I should stay, saying, it could not prolong his life
to neglect his duty; and repeating the following passage out of
Sarpedon's speech [12.310–28: Granville quoted in Greek]:

My friend, if by surviving this battle we were to be ageless and immortal, I should not fight myself in the foremost rank, nor should I urge you into the war where men win glory. But as it is, since countless fates of death stand over us, and no mortal may escape or avoid them, let us go forward.

His Lordship repeated the last word, (that is, in English, "let us go forward"), several times with a calm and determinate resignation; and, after a serious pause of some minutes, he desired to hear the Treaty read, to which he listened with great attention, and recovered spirits enough to declare the approbation of a dying statesman (I use his own words) "on the most glorious war, and most honourable peace, this nation ever saw".'

Secondly, the idea that the supreme subject, in writing of the past, is warlike achievement and suffering, was one which had a decisive impact on the writing of history. Herodotus, the 'father of history', begins his great work: 'This is the history of Herodotus of Halicarnassus, written so that remembrance of the actions of men shall not be lost with time, and so that great and wonderful deeds, both by the Greeks and by the barbarians, shall not lose their glory . . .'. He takes it for granted that his subject, and the 'great deeds', should be a great war. His successor Thucydides, the pioneer of scientific history, also took a great war as his subject; and he supports his choice with the argument that 'this war was drawn out to great length, and more disasters came upon Greece in the course of it than in any comparable period of time. Never were so many cities sacked and laid waste . . .'. Through the Roman historians, Livy and Tacitus, this conception of history as essentially military and political was to be dominant until the twentieth century. Nor has this been true only of the writers of history but also of its makers. We have ample evidence that Alexander the Great, who was said to sleep with the *Iliad* under his head, was consciously inspired by the example of Achilles, and that his reckless courage and impulsive generosity were in part a deliberate imitation. The heroic interpretation given to war fits with Homeric precedent. Alexander in turn became the model for Caesar and so for Charlemagne and Napoleon; a scarlet thread through the history of Europe goes back, in the end, to the *Iliad*.

That consequence was, perhaps, not entirely fortunate; another, which can be regarded as epoch-making in an unambiguously good sense, was the effect of the Homeric impartiality. Both Trojans and Greeks speak the same language, pray to the same gods, respect the same values; Hector and his wife Andromache are in some ways the most sympathetic characters in the poem, and it is with the King of Troy that Achilles shares that great vision of common humanity. The Trojans started the war and they have characteristic faults of over-confidence and frivolity, but there are no villains in the *Iliad*. The contrast is great with the presentation of history in the ancient traditions of the Levant; no Assyrian or Egyptian chronicler is concerned with the human qualities of the national enemy, any more than any Old Testament writer sets out to record 'great and wonderful deeds' both of the Chosen People and of their opponents, Canaanites or Philistines. To these chroniclers the idea of impartiality or dispassionate enquiry would have seemed an absurdity, and the point of their work was to justify and glorify their own people. History, in our sense, is a Greek invention, and the *Iliad* was vital to it.

It is no less vital to poetry. A play like Shakespeare's *Henry the Fifth*, with its heroic Englishmen and ignoble Frenchmen, shows the limitations of poetic power, however brilliant, without this perception of shared humanity. In the words of Professor Northrop Frye:

It is hardly possible to overestimate the importance for Western Literature of the *Iliad*'s demonstration that the fall of an enemy, no less than that of a friend or leader, is tragic and not comic. With the *Iliad*, once for all, an objective and disinterested element enters into the poet's vision of human life. Without this element, poetry is merely instrumental to various social aims, to propaganda, to amusement, to devotion, to instruction: with it, it acquires the authority that since the *Iliad* it has never lost, an authority based, like the authority of science, on the vision of nature as an impersonal order.
(*Anatomy of Criticism*, Princeton, 1957, 319)

Another problem of heroism is also already apparent in Homer: how does the prowess and self-assertion of the heroic individual relate to the interest and well-being of society as a whole? No line is more famous than that which tells us of Peleus' instruction to his son Achilles 'always to excel and to outstrip all others' (11.784). A band of men all of whom are heroes will not easily act in harmony, as the dearest wish of each of them must be to win pre-eminence and glory for himself. The warrior is of supreme value to these early societies, because they are constantly vulnerable and depend for their existence on the courage of their fighting men. The reward of the warrior is honour, but the demands of individual honour will often conflict with those of the community. Achilles vindicates his affronted honour by withdrawing from the fighting, and his comrades suffer disasters in his absence. Hector could have avoided the fatal duel with Achilles by retreating in time into Troy, and his parents implore him to do so. 'Come within the wall,' calls Priam, 'that you may preserve the men and women of Troy' (22.56). But Hector will not; he committed a strategic mistake last night by ordering the Trojan forces to bivouac out on the plain instead of going safely back to Troy, and that enabled Achilles, on his return to battle, to inflict a disastrous defeat and heavy losses. Now we see him argue the case with himself, as he stands outside the wall and Achilles approaches:

Ay me, if I go within the gates and the walls Polydamas will be the first to reproach me. He told me to lead the Trojans to the city before this night of disaster, when god-like Achilles rose up, but I would not yield to him; indeed it would have been much better. And now that I have lost the army by my folly, I am ashamed to face the men of Troy and the Trojan women in their trailing robes, lest someone, a lesser man than I, should say 'Hector trusted in his own strength and lost the army.' So will they speak; then it would be far better for me to face Achilles and either slay him before we part, or die myself gloriously before the city. (22.99–110)

The hero is trapped by the logic of his heroism. Striving always to excel, he finds that he cannot accept loss of face, even to preserve the men and women of Troy; and the death of Hector means the ruin of his country. Such tragedies as those of

Coriolanus, or Roland refusing to blow his horn for help at Roncesvalles, are akin to those of the *Iliad*.

What perhaps marks off the *Iliad* in particular is the fullness with which both sides are presented. This is not a romantic work which glorifies the magnificent individual and disregards the human cost, nor is it an anti-heroic sermon. We see that Hector and Achilles are great because they are heroes, that by accepting the weight of that role they raise human nature to its highest power, engage the gods in human life, and enable us to understand the world. But we are not spared the consequence for Achilles of his heroic stubbornness, which is not only the damage he does to his community but also the loss of his own dearest friend. And when Hector has died gloriously before the city we experience to the full the bereavement and despair of his country, his parents, and his wife. When Patroclus is dead, Achilles curses the anger which kept him sitting idle by the ships, 'and I did not help Patroclus or all my other comrades who were slain by god-like Hector.' Passionate impatience when dishonoured is part of the make-up of the hero, but by yielding to it Achilles has brought himself to a position where he can wish only to avenge Patroclus and die (18.98 ff.).

Hector, too, has a vision of the consequences of his courage and prowess. When his wife tries to restrain his boldness, he replies that self-respect must urge him into the front rank,

'for I have learned always to be brave and to fight in the forefront of the Trojans, maintaining my father's great glory and my own. Well do I know this in my heart: there will be a day when mighty Troy shall be destroyed, and Priam and the people of Priam of the ash-wood spear. But I am not so much grieved for the suffering of Troy hereafter, not even for that of Hecuba and King Priam, nor for my many brave brothers who shall fall in the dust at the hands of their enemies, as much as I am for you, when some Achaean warrior shall take you away, weeping, robbed of your freedom. Then you will work at the loom for a mistress in Argos, and fetch water from the spring of Messeis or Hypereia, sorely unwilling and under grievous constraint. . . . As for me, may I be dead and under the earth before I hear you shrieking as you are dragged away.' So spoke shining Hector and reached out to take his son, but the child shrank back crying into the bosom of his nurse, terrified by the sight of his own father, afraid of the bronze and the horsehair plume which he saw nodding grimly above his helmet. Then the father and mother laughed aloud, and Hector took off his helmet and laid it glittering on the ground, and he kissed his son and dandled him in his arms . . . (6.444 ff.)

Hector sees the whole cost of heroism and is still prepared to pay it, and the poet has included in this poignantly human scene a moving symbol of the dilemma of the warrior. The devoted husband must draw the courage to fight for his wife from the very hope that when disaster comes for her he will not be there; and to protect his infant son the loving father must turn into an inhuman figure in armour of bronze, who terrifies the child whom he dies to defend.

3 The Odyssey

The ancient Greeks regarded the *Iliad* as the greater of the Homeric poems, and the writer of this book shares that view. It is the *Iliad* which was quoted more, which was the subject of a greater volume of scholarly work, and which did more to form the Greek conception of the world and of man. It is a tragic work, whereas the *Odyssey* is an adventure story which ends happily, with the good rewarded and the wicked punished. The tragic view of human life is, alas, more deeply true than the view which sees straightforward poetic justice in the working-out of events, and that is in part why the *Odyssey* cannot equal the insights of the *Iliad*, rather as the optimistic assumptions and simple moral contrasts of a novel like *Nicholas Nickleby* make it impossible for it to have the profundity of one like *War and Peace*. But the *Odyssey* has great attractions of its own, and it is noteworthy that E. V. Rieu's Penguin translation of the *Odyssey* has had an enormous sale, far greater than that of his *Iliad*. One might say that this poem has more of the qualities of a novel, and indeed it is the ultimate ancestor of the novel in Europe.

There were other poems about the adventurous return journeys of Achaean heroes from Troy. These seem to have been comparatively short and simple works, on a much smaller scale than the *Odyssey*, which at its opening makes a conscious claim to be the last of the Return stories: 'then all the others, as many as had escaped sheer destruction, were at home, got clear of war and sea, but one man alone ...' (i.11–13). The poet seems to have had the intention of creating one very large poem, of the same order of size as the *Iliad*, which should sum up and replace the various poems on Returns. Many considerations of language, ideas, and structure, suggest to most modern scholars that the *Odyssey* was composed rather later than the *Iliad* and was influenced by it. In antiquity the two poems were almost universally ascribed to the same man, a view now held by very few of those who have worked on the question; but one influential opinion was that the *Iliad* was the work of the poet's youth, the *Odyssey* that of his old age, which perhaps has something in common with the separatist view which prevails today. It fits with it that the poem seems to make a point of including an account of the important events between the end of the *Iliad* and the beginning of the *Odyssey*: in book twenty-four we hear of the funeral of Achilles, in book eleven of the suicide of Ajax, in book four of the Wooden Horse and the sack of Troy, in book three of the Achaeans' departure from Troy, in book four of the adventurous journeys of Menelaus; above all the disastrous return of Agamemnon, a terrible warning of what might have happened to Odysseus, is repeatedly dwelt upon. It is likely enough that the poet of the *Odyssey* was roused by the existence of the *Iliad* to rival its great size in his own work.

The simple narrative of the return home of a hero has been greatly expanded. First, Odysseus' son Telemachus is promoted to the status of an important actor; the first four books deal with his adventures, first at home in Ithaca and then on his journey to Pylos and Sparta in quest of news of his father, while Odysseus himself does not appear until book five. This is a bold conception and might have produced a spectacular anticlimax, but the poet manages to create an effective crescendo of expectation. On Ithaca nobody has heard tidings of Odysseus for twenty years. For all that time there has been no meeting of the citizens in official council; his son assumes that his white bones are perishing in the rain or tossing in the sea, but all action is at a standstill until his fate is known one way or the other. Roused by Athena to go on a journey in search of news, Telemachus comes first to the court of Nestor, old and wise, and he has not seen Odysseus since the Achaeans sailed from Troy ten years before. After a long journey by land he comes to Menelaus in Sparta, who tells him that far away, off the coast of Egypt, he met a god who told him that Odysseus was held on an island by a goddess. This long series of scenes allows us to see the effect of the hero's absence upon his family, his community, and his friends; and it is constructed so as to show us how utterly cut off and lost he is – even at the ends of the earth only a god can tell where he is hidden. It is from that position that Odysseus must return.

We saw earlier that the plot of the *Odyssey* is complex where that of the *Iliad* is simple: Telemachus and Odysseus are described in their separate movements, and then they are united. But the complexity of the *Odyssey* goes far deeper than that. The visits to Nestor and Menelaus, in books three and four, enable the poet to include scenes of heroic domesticity – Nestor with his sons, and Menelaus at home with Helen, very much a great lady and in no way in disgrace for her escapade with Paris, or for the deaths which followed in the Trojan War. We see these glamorous and interesting people through the eyes of the dazzled Telemachus, who at first is so shy that he can hardly speak to Nestor, and the epic allows itself to come close to the comedy of manners as it depicts these encounters in which, of course, nothing really 'heroic', no 'great deeds', can happen. We shall have more to say of this later.

Another complexity is introduced by the device of making Odysseus narrate his own earlier adventures to the Phaeacians, in books nine to twelve. Stories like that of the outwitting of the One-Eyed Giant occur in folk-tales everywhere, and they could as readily have been told of any adventurer as of Odysseus; in fact, they have more in common with Sinbad the Sailor than with Achilles and Hector. The return of Odysseus is thus expanded by material of a very different type, and that had its consequences for the central aspects of the poem. The *Odyssey* is less reticent than the *Iliad* in admitting magical and supernatural events, although it is still austere by the standards of other early epics, in Greece or elsewhere; but the poet is careful to put the more bizarre and fantastic stories into the mouth of his characters, rather than vouching for their truth himself. It is Odysseus who tells us of the Cyclops, and of Circe turning men into pigs, and of the flesh of the Cattle of the Sun mooing on the spits as it is roasted; and King Alcinous says of his narrative, 'We do not think you are a deceiver or a liar, Odysseus, as the black earth bears many men who tell many lies. Your tale has form, and your mind is noble, and you have told your story skilfully, like a regular singer ...' (xi.362–8). The compliment is an ambiguous one, and deliberately so. Odysseus is even given the supreme accolade of a hero: he descends to the world of the dead, a motif which belongs more properly to Heracles, greatest of all heroes, and to Orpheus, supernatural singer who prevailed over death itself. The poet of the *Odyssey* produces some effective scenes of pathos, when the hero meets the shade of his mother and of his friends who died at Troy, but the episode as a whole is rather lightly attached to the poem. It is evident that the intention is to give Odysseus every heroic experience.

In the second half of the poem, once Odysseus has returned to Ithaca, expansion of a different sort is detectable, and the reader feels at moments that bulk is being sought for its own sake. Several scenes recur more than once in very similar form, as when Odysseus is jeered at by the maids and when suitors throw things at him. More seriously, there appears to be a wavering between two versions of the plot. As the main line of the poem goes, Odysseus does not reveal his identity to his wife until after he has got the bow into his hands and slain the suitors, but there are a number of moments when we seem to see, just below the surface and almost breaking through, a version in which he made himself known to her earlier, and she gave him the bow in the knowledge that he would use it in revenge. The tendency of recent scholarship has been to minimise these difficulties and to see in them a coherent poetic purpose, but it remains difficult, in this area, not to suspect the presence of different and incompatible accounts, as if our poem were drawing upon several substantial poems now lost.

The inclusion of events of a fairy-tale sort, ogres and monsters, has consequences for the heroism of the hero. In the cave of the Cyclops, or confronted with the magician Circe, the straightforward action of an Achilles is impossible; one cannot excel when menaced by supernatural power. Odysseus is a new

sort of hero, the survivor. Disguise, deception, endurance –
these are the qualities he needs to survive. In the *Iliad* Achilles
spoke for a simpler heroism when he said, and we notice that he
said it to Odysseus, 'I hate that man like the gates of hell who
hides one thing in his heart and says another' (9.312), and,
quite consistently, when he is instructed by Zeus to surrender
Hector's body to Priam he tells Priam so in so many words
(24.560–2), making no attempt to claim the credit for himself.
By contrast, Odysseus introduces himself to the Phaeacians
with the words, 'I am Odysseus, Laertes' son, famous all over
the world for my tricks' (ix.19), and his patron goddess Athena
congratulates him on being 'practised in deceits' beyond all
men, as she herself excels the gods in wit and scheming
(xiii.291–9). It is in harmony with this that Calypso, when she
is ordered by Zeus to let Odysseus go, never tells him why she is
doing it, implying that it is her own kind heart, and Odysseus
never knows (v.160–91, vii.262). When Achilles has slain
Hector, he cries, 'Come, let us sing a paean as we go back to the
ships, sons of the Achaeans: "We have won, a great victory; we
have killed the noble Hector, whom the Trojans adored in Troy
like a god" ' (22.391–4). In the more secretive world of the
Odyssey, Odysseus checks the old servant who starts a cry of
triumph over the bodies of the suitors: 'Rejoice in your heart,
old nurse, and control it, and raise no cry: it is an unholy thing
to exult over slain men' (xxii.411–12).

In the *Odyssey* one is surrounded and menaced by deceit. In
his wanderings Odysseus meets Circe, who welcomes all comers
sweetly, gives them food and drink, and then transforms them
into animals; and the Sirens, who call him by name and sing to
him, but who would waste him away to death if he listened to
them. In Ithaca the loyal retainer Eumaeus was born a prince
but was stolen away as a child by a treacherous nursemaid and
sold into slavery, and he has spent his life as a swineherd.
Penelope is made miserable by vagabonds and liars who tell her
false tales about her absent husband in order to get things out of
her (xv.403 ff., xiv.122 ff.: we observe that Eumaeus is so cyni-
cal as to say to the disguised Odysseus himself, 'You too, old

man, would invent a tale quickly enough, if someone were to
give you a cloak and a tunic to wear'). Against such a world one
must defend oneself by self-control and patience, and not least
by disguise. Odysseus moves among the Phaeacians from book
six to the opening of book nine, incognito and mysterious;
when the bard Demodocus sings the tale of the Wooden Horse
and Odysseus' own role in the taking of Troy, Odysseus weeps
in silence but resists the temptation to reveal his identity. In the
same way he moves about his own house in disguise from book
seventeen to book twenty-one, and resists the temptation to
unmask before the time, even when he is insulted by his own
maids or when he sees Penelope weep. His heart howls like a
dog within him, but he succeeds in subduing it:

Endure, my heart: you have endured a worse thing, on the day when
the Cyclops, irresistible in strength, was devouring your brave comrades. Yet you bore it, until your cunning brought you out of the
cave where you expected to die. (xx.18–21)

Even the war with Troy comes to wear a very different appearance in this poem. Odysseus, we read, entered Troy in
disguise and slew many Trojans by guile (iv.240 ff.), and he got
the Wooden Horse into the city by a trick (viii.494). Nestor
even describes the whole war by saying 'For nine years we were
busy about them, devising their ruin by tricks of every kind'
(iii.119) – a conception quite different from that in which the
heroic simplicity of Achilles and Ajax led the Achaean attack.
Odysseus' wife and son share his self-restraint. Penelope shows
her ability to conceal her real thoughts from the suitors, above
all in the famous story of the web. Announcing that she cannot
remarry before she has woven a handsome shroud for Odysseus' father Laertes, she undoes by night what she has woven
by day, and so keeps the suitors at bay for three years (ii.85 ff.).
In the end her self-control has become a habit which she cannot
break; brought face to face with her husband, the suitors dead,
she still finds it hard to believe in his identity (xxiii).

The gods who preside over this world have also changed
their nature. Gods now come, we are told, and move among

men in disguise, testing them to see whether they are virtuous or wicked. The king of the Phaeacians asks the disguised Odysseus if he is a god, and the more nervous of the suitors are alarmed when a violent spirit among them attacks the hero in his disguise as a beggar, pointing out that he could be a god (vii.199, xvii.485). And in fact Odysseus does behave like a god in this respect, announcing his intention of testing his servants by moving among them incognito (xvi.305); while in the end the destruction of the suitors is seen less as a heroic achievement than as a piece of divine justice. Penelope, hearing that they are dead, refuses to believe that her husband has returned and done it, and says

No, it is one of the immortals who has slain the haughty suitors, angered by their grievous insolence and their wickedness; they respected no man on earth, good or bad, who came among them, and therefore they have come to ruin through their own wantonness. (xxiii.63–7)

When Odysseus' old father Laertes hears that the suitors are slain, his response is to say, 'Father Zeus, in truth you gods are still on high Olympus, if the suitors have indeed paid for their crimes' (xxiv.351–2).

This is a very different way of being 'god-like' from the splendid self-assertion of the *Iliad*. The hero presents himself as an almost anonymous agent of divine justice, resembling gods who are no longer the serene and self-confident rulers of the world, with no need to justify their actions, but who have become almost anxious in defending themselves. At the very beginning of the poem Zeus speaks to Athena, and if we remember the divine scenes of the first book of the *Iliad*, with their extraordinary mixture of grandeur and frivolity, we must be struck by the difference here. Zeus is brooding on the fate of Aegisthus, the adulterous lover of Agamemnon's wife Clytemnestra, who seduced her and murdered her husband when he returned in triumph from Troy, only to be killed in his turn by Agamemnon's son Orestes. 'Alas,' says the father of gods and men,

How men reproach the gods. They say that it is from us that evil comes, while they of their own will, through their own wanton sin, incur suffering beyond what is ordained. Even so did Aegisthus take the wedded wife of Atreus' son, beyond what was ordained, and slay him when he came home, although he knew it was sheer ruin, for we had told him so beforehand. We sent Hermes the keen-sighted Argus-slayer, to tell him neither to kill the man nor to take his wife ... Now Aegisthus has paid for it all. (i.32–43)

Here is a representation of the divine which is applied with great consistency in the poem. Those who come to grief are sinners, who have brought it upon themselves; and they are explicitly warned before it is too late, but they choose to disregard the warning. The suitors are even sent an eerie vision of their own destruction, but they choose to disregard it (xx.345–71). No doubt the old tale of the returning hero who, given up for dead, arrives just in time to prevent the forced marriage of his wife and the loss of his kingdom – a story which is found all over the world – made no great fuss about the disappearance of the hero's companions. It is vital for the story that he shall come home alone and have to face great odds, as we see if we try to imagine an *Odyssey* in which Odysseus reaches Ithaca with twelve shiploads of warriors at his back from Troy. The suitors, too, must have been slaughtered simply because they were suitors, outraging the position and the rights of the hero by their presumption. But in our *Odyssey* all this has become morally questionable, and the poet is careful to assure us that Odysseus did all that he could to save his men, who brought their own ruin on themselves despite his efforts.

Much suffering did he endure on the deep, struggling for his own life and the return of his comrades. But even so he could not save his comrades, although he desired it: they perished through their own wantonness, the fools; they devoured the cattle of the god of the Sun, and he took away their home-coming. (i.4–9)

The poor comrades had been warned that the cattle of the Sun must not be touched, but under the pressure of imminent starvation they gave in; the hero, meanwhile, lay fast asleep – as he must do also when the incorrigible sailors open the leather bag in which the winds have been given to Odysseus by the lord of the winds, Aeolus, and the resulting storm blows them far away from Ithaca, which is already in view (xii.338, x.31). These untimely naps on the part of Odysseus are the rather transparent means which the poet has found to separate his hero from the criminal blunders of the men whose doom is to be explained and justified. As for the suitors, their guilt is increased by a device which arises naturally from the expansion of the role of Telemachus. As the young prince becomes an active figure, the suitors are driven to plan his death, and they actually lay an ambush for him, to murder him on his return from Sparta. A justification for their destruction is put forward which goes beyond what satisfied a simpler age: they are not just disloyal vassals and sinners against a hero, but in intention they are murderers.

Hero and gods alike are now justified by an explicitly moral standard. In the *Iliad* there are no villains, but the *Odyssey* is full of the contrast of moral black and white. The suitors are villains; of Odysseus' servants some are virtuous and loyal retainers who are rewarded (the old nurse Eurycleia, the swineherd Eumaeus, and the oxherd Philoetius), others are traitors who die a humiliating death (Melanthius the goatherd, the maids who slept with the suitors). In heaven, the robust clashes between gods which enlivened the *Iliad*, and which were to distress later theologians, give place to more decorous behaviour: gods do not oppose each other, and Athena tells Odysseus that she avoided defending him when Poseidon was persecuting him because 'I did not want to fight with my uncle Poseidon' (xiii.341). In fact few gods appear in the action at all, Odysseus' patron Athena having things very much her own way with her constant interventions, and we are generally given the impression of one undivided and righteous divine will.

The remarkable exception to this is the lively and improper story which the bard Demodocus performs to entertain the court of Phaeacia. He sings of the intrigue of Aphrodite, goddes of love, who is married to the lame craftsman god Hephaestus, with Ares the god of war. The cuckolded husband, informed of what is going on by the all-seeing Sun, sets a trap about his bed, a net of strong chains, as thin as cobwebs, invisible to the eye. The lovers, deceived by Hephaestus into thinking that he has gone off on a journey, go to bed together, and the chains hold them fast. The husband calls in all the gods to witness the shameful scene and demands back the price he had paid to her father for marriage with this unfaithful wife. All the gods come, though the goddesses stay away out of modesty, 'and unquenchable laughter arose among the blessed gods as they looked at the device of cunning Hephaestus'. He is prevailed upon to release the humiliated pair, who go off to their special shrines, he to Thrace, she to Cyprus (viii.266–369).

In this story, so popular with later ages, the first appearance of the frivolous treatment of Olympian amours which was to blossom in the *Metamorphoses* of Ovid and in the imagination of countless writers and artists of the Renaissance, we see as it were that whole side of the gods of the *Iliad* which was less than straightforwardly dignified and moral, compressed and intensified into a single episode of the *Odyssey*. But the poet is still careful to put the unedifying tale into the mouth of a character, not into his own; and that character is entertaining the Phaeacians, a people with superhuman privileges but also one not taken quite seriously by the poet. There the queen is the important person, we are told, not the king; and they boast of themselves that 'We are not great boxers or wrestlers, but we are swift runners and seamen, and we love always the feast and music and dancing, and changes of raiment, and warm baths, and bed' (viii.246–9). This is the kind of song the Phaeacians *would* like. But we still can see, even here, the serious theme of the *Odyssey* underlying the tale. Hephaestus, Aphrodite, and Ares form a triangle analogous to that of Menelaus, Helen, and Paris, and, more tragically, to that of Agamemnon, Clytemnestra, and Aegisthus. The triangle of Odysseus, Penelope, and one of the suitors, might have taken the same form. On earth such a story must end with violent death; in heaven the serious suffering of men is transposed into laughter, there can be no death, and Aphrodite arises from her disgrace and goes off to Cyprus, to Paphos, where she has a precinct and an altar fragrant with incense. There the Graces bathed her and anointed her with unguent imperishable, such as is laid upon the everlasting gods, and they clothed her in lovely garments, a wonder to see. (viii.363–6)

We have seen that the epic hero Odysseus is plunged into adventures and situations in which the heroism of an Achilles would be impossible, and that a new heroism of patience and cunning is thus to some extent forced upon him. Despite this, he still remains the hero of an epic; and the two conceptions produce, at times, strange and complex effects when they are brought close together. When the Cyclops comes into his cave and finds there Odysseus and twelve of his men,

Our hearts died within us for fear of his deep voice and his monstrous shape; yet still I answered him, saying 'We are Achaeans wandering home from Troy, driven by all manner of winds over the great deeps of the sea. We seek our way home, but we have come another road and other ways; such must be the will of Zeus. We boast that we are the men of Agamemnon, Atreus' son, whose fame is now greatest under heaven, so mighty a city he has sacked, and destroyed many people. But as for us we come here to your knees, to see if you will give us a stranger's gift or any other present, as is the due of strangers. At least, sir, have respect for the gods – we are suppliants to you, and Zeus is the avenger of suppliants and strangers, Zeus the god of the stranger, who goes with travellers and enforces their due. (ix.259–71)

In this touching speech we hear the two sides of poor Odysseus' character and his situation. The giant terrifies him, but he still speaks up bravely, like a hero, and sounds convincing enough with his boast of his heroic connections and the glorious deed in which he has borne a part. But then the speech takes a different turn, a mere plea for their lives. The glory of Troy and of Agamemnon is no use against an ogre, and the juxtaposition makes the boast sound strangely pathetic.

The same thing happens repeatedly in the adventures. Circe predicts to Odysseus the perils that await him; when she tells him of Scylla and Charybdis, the six-headed monster on one side and the fearsome maelstrom on the other, Odysseus asks how he can punish Scylla for the damage she will do to his crew. Circe replies 'Headstrong man, again your thoughts are of fighting and of struggle; will you not yield even to immortal gods? Scylla is not mortal but an immortal bane, terrible, grievous, and savage, not to be fought with. There is no defence: it is best to flee from her.' But when Odysseus comes to the spot, 'Then I forgot the hard instruction of Circe, who forbade me to put on my armour, and I put my famous armour on and took two long spears in my hands and climbed up on to the prow of the ship . . .'. But while the hero and his men are intent upon the peril from Charybdis, suddenly from the other side Scylla snatches six of the crew.

They called to me by name for the last time in their agony . . . There Scylla devoured them outside her cave, while they shrieked and stretched out their hands to me in their sore death-throes. That was the most pitiful sight of all that my eyes have seen in my labours, searching out the paths of the sea. (xii.112 ff., 226–59)

Odysseus tries to be a hero and to fight even against supernatural perils, but again the effect is only one of pathos. The old heroism is disappearing over the horizon.

We can observe no less than three layers in the episode of the enchantress Circe. In the first, which is the simplest and has most clearly the character of a folk tale, Odysseus is saved from being turned into a pig like his companions, by being given a magical antidote to her magical drug. Hermes meets him and gives him the supernatural plant 'which gods call "moly", but which is hard for mortal men to dig up; but gods can do all things'. He tells the hero that 'she will not be able to bewitch you, for the powerful herb that I shall give you will prevent her'. What Odysseus is to do, when Circe has tried her magic on him in vain, is to rush on her with drawn sword: to behave, that is, like a man of war. But when he has done all this and Circe has called him to her bed and sworn an oath not to harm him, she says to him,

Who are you, and whose son? Where is your city and where are your parents? I marvel that you drank the magic drink and were not bewitched. There is no other man who is proof against this charm, once it has passed his lips; but your mind within you is superior to enchantment. In truth you must be Odysseus, and Hermes often told me that you would come here on your way from Troy. (x.325–32)

No mention here of the magic plant, which we never hear of again after its presentation, nor of the martial heroism of the drawn sword. It is by his own mental quality that Odysseus has prevailed against enchantment, and we seem to see here the successive stages by which a fairy story of a witch in a wood has been made first heroic and then something more sophisticated and inward – the mind conquers and is recognised by its opponent for what it is.

The focus of attention does more than simply move from the heroic fighting man; it also widens. The *Odyssey* is keenly interested in many things which the more austere manner of the *Iliad* excluded from serious attention. We have seen that servants play an important role in this poem. Odysseus on his first return to Ithaca goes straight to the hut of Eumaeus, the loyal swineherd; Eumaeus, his hut and his dogs are all lovingly described, and the poem lingers over them for three books before the hero sets off for his own palace (xiv–xvi). We are told what the servants of the suitors are like, how Odysseus' maid-servants behave, how demoralised loyal retainers become when they cannot speak face to face with the mistress, have something to eat and drink, and go off carrying some little present (xv.376). We have here the ultimate ancestor of the pastoral, with its interest in simple country folk and their concerns.

The *Odyssey* is also interested in professional singers, both among the Phaeacians and at home in Ithaca. The blind singer Demodocus is one of the unforgettable persons of the poem. It has a keen and informed eye for work. We see Odysseus build a raft on Calypso's island, and he tells us how he built his great double bed, which incorporates the trunk of an olive tree as a bed-post, so that the bed is immovable – 'round this I built the room with stones close-set, and I roofed it and added doors ... then I rough-hewed the trunk upwards from the root and smoothed it with the adze ... I made it beautiful with inlaid work of gold and silver and ivory ...' (xxiii.192–200). He boasts that he is an excellent hand at ploughing and at reaping corn, as well as fighting (xviii.366–75), whereas in the *Iliad*, in the description of the scenes on the shield of Achilles, we read of the reapers hard at work, while the king 'stands among them, holding a sceptre, rejoicing at heart' (18.556). Clearly we have a less high-flown conception in the *Odyssey*, in which the ideal of a man includes not only war-like prowess but also skill and pride in husbandry; work has become dignified, and the dandies of Phaeacia and the idle suitors are viewed with sharp irony.

It is hardly going too far to say of the *Odyssey* that it has a real interest in politics. In the *Iliad* the kings are kings, and it is for the rest to do what they are told. In the first book of the *Iliad* King Agamemnon simply ignores the view expressed by the army in assembly, that Chryseis should be given back to her father, and it is evident that he is within his rights in doing so, although the result shows that he made an error of judgement, and that involves humiliation. In the second book the assembly of the Achaeans is a disorderly affair. The troops are mustered with difficulty, and as soon as Agamemnon has finished speaking they simply bolt for the ships. Odysseus restores order by drastic methods, and in a unique passage one of the lower orders speaks out, in violent criticism of the king. The poet gives a hateful description of him:

Thersites alone still chattered on, that prattler uncontrolled, whose thoughts were many and jumbled, all in confusion, to attack the chiefs and to raise a laugh among the Achaeans. He was the ugliest man who came to Troy: bandy he was, and lame of one foot, his two shoulders rounded, arched down across his chest. His head was pointed, and a scanty stubble sprouted on it. (2.212–19)

His shrill attack on the king, in which he echoes much of Achilles' angry speeches in book one, disgusts the whole army, the poet assures us, and when he is beaten and silenced by Odysseus everybody is delighted. For men of the people Odysseus has a firm line: 'Sit quiet and listen to your betters, you who are no fighter, not reckoned with in war or in council. We cannot all be kings: not good is a multitude of masters; let there be

one master, one king' (2.200–5). And there is no more trouble
with the army, nor does anybody attempt to speak except
Odysseus, Nestor, and Agamemnon.

This scene is virtually the only sign in the *Iliad* that there can
be anything more to political life than implicit obedience to the
orders of a kingly class ordained by Zeus. It is emphatic in an
uncharacteristic way, and the reader is tempted to infer that in
reality demagogues were not always hated and rejected by the
common man, as Thersites is; but that is not much to go on. In
the *Odyssey* politics are more developed and more interesting.
We must of course allow for the fact that the *Iliad* describes an
army in the field, the *Odyssey* a regular state, but we observe
that in Troy, too, the popular will can be ignored (3.154–60,
7.346–64). The assembly of the men of Ithaca in the second
book, the first for twenty years, is far more like an assembly in
real life, with no less than seven speakers and a proper pro-
cedure; and again in the last book the relatives of the dead
suitors hold a meeting at which different views are expressed
and emotions aroused (ii.1–259, xxiv.412–71). The purpose of
the first meeting, called by Telemachus, is to mobilise public
opinion against the suitors, and this weapon is formidable
enough to alarm them; after the failure of their attempt to
ambush him, one of the more violent of them urges that they
must now kill him at once, 'before he calls the people together
in assembly. He will tell them all the story, and they will disap-
prove; they may do us harm and drive us out into exile'
(xvi.376–82).

At the assembly of the suitors' kinsmen Odysseus is accused
of losing his men as well as slaying the suitors; a commander is
to be held responsible for what happens to his subordinates
(xxiv.427), and this is a justification not merely for carping
criticism of the sort which Hector feared in the *Iliad* (22.106)
but for violent deposition. On the other side, Odysseus' sup-
porters argue that he was 'gentle and kind' and 'as kind as a
father', and so he has a right to the devotion of his people. The
position of the king is now at risk among aspiring nobles, both
in Ithaca, where it is in the suitors' view an open question who

should succeed Odysseus, Telemachus himself saying 'There are many kings in the island of Ithaca' (i.394), and also among the Phaeacians, where the king seems little more than first among equals. No doubt this mirrors the historical situation as the old hereditary monarchies in Greek cities were replaced by aristocracies. In the poem, it focuses attention on questions of loyalty and obligation, both within the king's own household and in its relations with ambitious noblemen, and with the greater interest in ordinary people goes a greater feeling of their power: Odysseus himself is anxious to explore the state of feeling among his servants before he reveals himself (xvi.301–7). On his journeys, too, he has trouble with a turbulent subordinate: Eurylochus, a cousin of his own, repeatedly tries to get his men to take a different line from that of the hero (x.429, xii.278).

Questions of status are at the heart of the poem. When Odysseus is telling a false story of his own life, it is natural for him to produce one which presents him as the illegitimate son of a rich man, favoured by his father but deprived of his inheritance by his legitimate brothers after the old man's death; a tough fighter, who has married the daughter of a wealthy man because of his personal prowess, he takes to a piratical existence (xiv.199 ff.). In another of his inventions he claims to be in exile because he has killed the son of a Cretan king, who tried to deprive him of his share of the booty of Troy 'because I would not truckle to his father and serve among his men, but commanded men of my own' (xiii.260–6). Whereas in the *Iliad* the hero needs to contend only with other heroes, risking his life but preserving his supremacy, the *Odyssey* is keenly aware of the unheroic struggles for position and property, and brings out every detail of them.

The poem has time also for the weak and the ordinary, whereas the *Iliad* is always looking to the outstanding. The limelight can fall upon such a character as Elpenor, one of Odysseus' men, who gets drunk and sleeps on the roof, then forgets where he is and falls off and breaks his neck. 'He was no great fighter in war, nor were his wits of the firmest,' is

Odysseus' comment on him (x.552). Yet he is allowed to appear to Odysseus among the dead and beg for honourable burial:

Leave me not unwept and unburied when you return, nor turn your back on me, lest the gods be angry for my sake. Burn me with my armour, all that I have, and heap a mound over me by the shore of the grey sea, the grave of an unlucky man, that those to come may hear of me; and then on the grave plant my oar, with which I rowed while I was alive among my comrades. (xi.72–8)

There is a full and sympathetic treatment of beggars, and the poet knows that a beggar is likely to do better in the town than out in the country (xvii.18). Even the poor servant woman who grinds corn at the mill and is the weakest of those who are set to this, the least enviable of all servile tasks, so that after the others have finished and gone off to bed she is still toiling to complete her allotted work, attracts the eye of the poet, who allows her a prayer to Zeus for the destruction of the suitors; their demands have worn her out (xx.105). That they have overworked a servant is a part of their offence. In a very famous scene he makes effective use of the pathos of an old dog, in his day a hunter, but now thrown out to die on the dung-hill because his master is far away. Recognising his master after twenty years, the dog Argus wags his tail and drops his ears, but has not the strength to approach him; Odysseus conceals a tear from Eumaeus, and as they pass the dog dies (xvii.290 ff.). The episode is justly celebrated and so skilfully managed as to avoid sentimentality, while extracting from the situation all that can be got out of it, but the *Iliad*, we feel, would not think it sufficiently heroic to be included.

In the *Odyssey* it goes without saying that Nausicaa, a king's daughter, helps with the washing. A charming incident is made of her going off to the sea-shore with her friends and a picnic; when the laundry is done they play ball on the beach (vi.1–118). Old Laertes, Odysseus' father, was always a keen gardener, and we hear how he gave his little son a row of fruit-trees for his own. Obviously the young Odysseus was to become responsible for them (xxiv.336). The poet gives a crowning instance of the difference between his conception of the hero and that of medi-

eval chivalry, in which the knightly class is defined by its absolute freedom from work and indeed by opposition to it in
principle, when he uses the weary ploughman as a simile for the
yearning of Odysseus for his home. On his last evening among
the Phaeacians, who have promised to take him home that
night, amid the pleasures of the feast and of the singing of
Demodocus,

Yet Odysseus turned his head often towards the brilliant sun, eager
for its setting; such was his yearning for his homeward journey. As
when a man longs for his evening meal, for whom all day long two
dark oxen have been dragging the jointed plough; it is welcome to
him when the sun goes down and he may go to his supper, while
his knees tremble as he goes: even so was the sunset welcome to
Odysseus. (xiii.28–35)

The poet feels no incongruity in such a comparison, and his
hero is not degraded by the idea of manual work. He is himself
no stranger to it.

The world of Odysseus also contains trade, largely in the
hands of Phoenicians, and piracy. The two are indeed not
always clearly distinguished; the Phoenicians who stole the
young Eumaeus were traders, but a little kidnapping and sel-
ling into slavery came easily to them. Heroic honour for the
Homeric poems is inseparable from possessions, and we recall
that both the anger of Achilles and the vengeance of Odysseus
were provoked by robbing the hero of something he owned;
while even for homicide satisfaction can be made by the pay-
ment of blood-money (9.632). But while Achilles shows his
extraordinary greatness of soul by rising above a keen interest in
the details of compensation, Odysseus goes to the other ex-
treme. Shipwrecked and alone, he has of course lost the
treasures which fell to his share at the sack of Troy, and he is
sharply aware of his loss and anxious to recoup it. We receive a
slight shock when he says to the Phaeacian king,

Lord Alcinous, outstanding leader of the people, if you were to bid
me stay here even for a year, and promised me my convoy home and
splendid gifts, even that would I choose. It would be much better for
me to come with a fuller hand to my own dear country; so I should

have more respect and love with all men who might see me after my return to Ithaca. (xi.355–61)

Later Greeks were a little offended by Odysseus' eye to profit, and that criticism is expressed within the poem itself; a young Phaeacian noble tells him that he is not like a man skilled in sport but

like a man who comes and goes in a benched ship, a captain of a trading vessel, with his mind on his cargo and his merchandise, and on the snatching of profit; you are not like an athlete. (viii.159–64)

This is a deadly insult, and at once Odysseus refutes it by performing a remarkable athletic feat, flinging a heavier discus far beyond the distance achieved by the Phaeacians with lighter ones, but we feel that the charge was not wholly without justice. Even the poet himself seems to feel satisfaction at the thought that in the end Odysseus comes home with more treasure than he originally brought away from Troy (v.36–40).

With this interest in trading goes an awareness of travel, and of foreign countries. Many stories are told which are about journeys to Egypt, for trade and plunder, or simply as a result of unfavourable winds. Odysseus and the poet share an interest in exotic places: at the beginning of the poem we are told that he 'saw many cities of men and learned their character' (i.3). When the hero reaches the island of the Cyclopes, there is another opposite where he moors his ships. He gives us a full and detailed account of it. Uninhabited and full of wild goats,

it is not poor but would bear every crop in its season. There are meadows by the shore of the grey sea, well-watered and soft; there vines might grow perennial. And there is smooth plough land, from which men might reap very deep crops in due season, for the soil beneath is rich. And there is a fine harbour for ships . . . At the head of the harbour is a spring of bright water . . . (ix.116 ff.)

We remember that in the eighth and seventh centuries BC Greek cities were establishing colonies all round the Eastern Mediterranean, and we seem to see in this passage something like a prospectus to attract settlers to a new site. The focus of the *Iliad*, intense but narrower, which had no need of foreign travel or elaborate economic activities to set the scene for heroic action and suffering, has opened up to include the origins of what would soon become the sciences of geography and ethnography. The restless Greek curiosity finds its first expression in the *Odyssey*, luring Odysseus into the Cyclops' cave (ix.174). The poet gives us an outline of the geography and history of Crete, and of such special features as the extraordinary fertility of sheep in North Africa (xix.172–80, iv.81–9); and he comments on the absence of communal life among the Cyclopes, who 'have no assembly and no laws' (ix.112).

The theme of a travelling hero who goes to different places and has adventures and love affairs, often going in disguise or unrecognised, was to be the original form of the Greek novel, which began to appear in the fourth century BC. These romances, whose surviving examples are nowadays little read, formed the background for those much more complex and entertaining works, the *Satyricon* of Petronius and Apuleius' *Metamorphoses*, or *Golden Ass*. From them the tradition came down to the first novels in the modern European languages, and such books as *Don Quixote* and *Tom Jones* are recognisably of the same origin.

Not the least important and interesting of the new subjects which interest the *Odyssey* is that of women. In the *Iliad* the portraits of women – Hecuba, Andromache, Helen – are completely satisfying, and one has no sense of the squeaky voice of the female impersonator. The goddesses, too, intervene in a spirit and manner clearly different from that of the gods, a difference which certainly does not mean that they are less active or less effective. But the women of the *Iliad*, like everything else in that highly concentrated poem, exist primarily to bring out the figure of the fighting man. Hecuba is the mother of warrior sons, the noble Hector and the less satisfactory Paris; what we see of her shows her as a mother. Andromache is the wife of the hero and the mother of his child. She is given enough vitality and depth to fill this role with memorable perfection; her hopes and fears, her wifely existence and its destruction, complete the depiction of the hero's life. If there were no Andromache and no child to risk one's life for, heroism would be both less necessary and less terrible. The thought of her suffering is the most tormenting of all the anxieties which Hector must carry into battle. Helen, too, is seen in her relationship with the two warriors, Hector and Paris, while the personality of poor Briseis, the captive woman who is taken from Achilles and who is thus at the heart of the action of the poem, is not developed at all.

In the *Odyssey*, by contrast, we find a whole gallery of contrasting female figures. Odysseus is entangled first with Circe and then with Calypso; among the Phaeacians he meets the princess Nausicaa and also her formidable mother Arete; the faithful wife Penelope waits for him at home, in a household whose strongest personality seems to be the devoted but not always submissive old nurse, Eurycleia. On his journeys he is directed and constantly supervised by the goddess Athena, whose attitude to him is much more intimate than that of goddesses to men in the *Iliad*. There have been those who have thought that the poem was actually the work of a woman, an idea first floated by Samuel Butler, but it is rather naïve to think that an interest in women necessarily suggests feminine authorship. It is perhaps more significant that it goes with the interest of the poem in concealed motives and opaque personalities. Even in the *Iliad* the most elaborate passage in which a character acts from a disguised motive is that of Hera seducing Zeus in book fourteen: she tells a false tale to Aphrodite in order to induce her to lend an irresistible cosmetic for the purpose, and then she goes off to Zeus and tells him, casually, that she is just off on a journey ... All this shows us the feminine way of going to work, achieving its ends by subtlety and indirection rather than the frontal assault of the simpler male.

For what all the women of the *Odyssey* have in common is a mysteriousness which the male characters fail to master. Calypso is a loving woman, who wishes to keep Odysseus on her island and marry him, but she is also a superhuman person, an immortal goddess, of whose anger he must be careful. The messenger god Hermes, sent by Zeus to tell her that she must let Odysseus go, is himself tactful in his approach. 'You ask me why I have come? Zeus made me come, much against my will; it is a long and disagreeable journey, but no god can cross or evade the will of Zeus. He says there is a man here with you ... his command is that you let him go' (v.97–115, paraphrased). The emphasis on the overwhelming power of Zeus conveys a warning to Calypso, but does it in an urbane way. As for Odysseus, the tactful god avoids any mention of the important fact, which is that she loves him and will for that reason find the command hard to obey. Calypso expresses her grief and indignation, making no bones of her love, and complaining of the double standard of heaven, which intervenes to prevent goddesses from enjoying the love of mortal men. But when she comes to tell Odysseus the news, she says to him 'Weep no more: I shall send you off with all my heart. Build a raft, and I shall send you a favourable wind, so that you may come safely to your home-land, if it be the gods' will, who are stronger than I am to plan and to fulfil.' The last words of this speech have a meaning for us which they have not for Odysseus; we know that they express her bitterness that the stronger power of the gods is forcing her to part with him, but of course he does not, and hears only that she will now voluntarily aid his departure.

Naturally surprised by this unexpected change of heart, Odysseus suspects a trick and makes her swear an oath that she means him no harm. She complies, smiling, and concludes 'For my mind is righteous and my heart in my bosom is not of iron; no, it is kindly' (v.190–1). She leads him to the cave, and Odysseus 'sat down on the chair from which Hermes had arisen', and the two eat together, he eating and drinking 'such things as mortal men consume', while she is served the nectar and ambrosia of the gods. The detail of the chair, again, is significant for us but not for Odysseus, who does not know that Hermes has just been there to force his release, while the different food which they eat together is a symbol of their fundamentally different nature: they do not belong together.

Their last conversation is described with great delicacy, and what is not said is very important. 'Are you so very anxious to sail straight away home? Then farewell. But if you knew all the sufferings that await you, then you would stay here with me and be immortal, for all your yearning to see your wife, for whom you long every day. I am not less beautiful than she, for I am a goddess and she but a mortal woman' (v.203–12). Such a speech is not easy to answer; to take a tactful farewell of a loving woman is never easy, and in this utterance of Calypso we hear her say, 'It is only for that wife of yours that you are leaving me – when I could do so much more for you! And her attractions do not compare with mine.' And behind that 'Stay with me!' Odysseus begins by emphasising her divinity; she is far above him. 'Dread goddess, be not angry with me. I know it is all true, that prudent Penelope is inferior to you in beauty and stature: she is mortal, you are deathless and ageless. But still I long to go home and see the day of my return. If I must suffer on the way, I have endured much before; let this be added to it.' He hastens to admit that Penelope is less attractive – it is not for her but for his home that he is yearning. The unspoken plea receives only an implicit answer, and the hero does what he can to reduce the hurt to her pride and allow her to keep her dignity.

Circe is a very different type. When her magic fails against Odysseus she at once invites him to her bed, but the circumspect hero suspects that she plans to 'make me weak and unmanned when I am naked' (x.341), and he binds her with a solemn oath, something which Hermes advised him to do, and which we feel was a very sensible precaution. They sleep together, Circe restores his men to their human shape, and for a year they live with her in the lap of luxury. It is his men, not Odysseus, who eventually feel that it is time to be going. Odysseus embraces her knees in the gesture of supplication and begs her to allow them to depart: 'My heart longs to go home, and so does that of my comrades, who break my heart with their lamentations round me, when you are not near' (x.484–6). The reply of the goddess is brisk: 'Do not stay in my house against your will . . .'. She makes the plans and gives them the provisions for their journey, which must be to the land of the dead. There is no scene of farewell, and as they go down to

their ship Circe passes them unseen to take them the black ewe
and ram which must be offered to the dead: 'Who can see a god
as he passes, if he does not choose?'

The immediate transition from hostility to the offer of her
bed is by human standards strange, belonging to the logic of
Grimm's fairy tales rather than real life, and it is never made
clear whether Circe, who has already recognised this stranger as
Odysseus, really would have done him some terrible mischief
but for her oath. Odysseus' men remain terrified of her, and the
hero himself approaches her gingerly, evidently not knowing
how she will react to the request that they be allowed to depart.
She is no tender Calypso, and her response is business-like,
but to the last she moves mysteriously, and Odysseus' final
rhetorical question – 'Who can see a god ... if he does not
choose?' – shows how little he felt confident of understanding
her.

The loving Calypso and the hard-boiled Circe represent two
types of women whom the heroic sailor may meet as he travels
about the world. Nausicaa is a third: the ingénue, with whom
everything remains only potential. The night that Odysseus is
to be cast up on the shore of her country, naked and battered,
she has a dream. A friend appears to her and says 'Nausicaa,
soon you will be getting married; the young noblemen of our
country are all asking for your hand. You will need clean
clothes, for yourself and to give to those who take you away.
Let us go down to the river and wash clothes tomorrow; ask
your father for a waggon and mules' (vi.25–40). Nausicaa asks
her father, saying merely that she has a great deal of washing to
do; for, the poet observes, 'she felt ashamed to mention lusty
marriage to her father, but he understood it all ...' (vi.65).
When Odysseus is woken from exhausted sleep by the shrill
cries of the girls, whose ball has gone into the sea, he faces an
awkward situation. Is he to make the standard gesture of supplication, embracing the knees of the princess, naked and caked
with brine as he is? He is prudent enough to decide that she
may not like this, and so he stands some way off and makes a
most courteous and elaborate speech, in which he compliments

her on her beauty ('are you a goddess?'), and lets her know that, despite appearances, he is a gentleman and has known better days ('when I went to Delos, with many followers at my back'). He ends by wishing her 'all her heart's desire': a home and a loving husband. No wonder that she accepts him, 'since you seem to be neither low nor foolish', and that she drops him a heavy hint – 'You must not appear with me, or people will say "Who is this tall handsome stranger with Nausicaa? Where did she find him? She will be marrying him next" ' (vi.275). Obediently Odysseus makes his own way into town, and when Nausicaa's father says to him that he has one fault to find with his daughter's handling of the affair, that she should have accompanied him into the town herself, Odysseus defends her with the white lie that she did tell him to come with her, but that he preferred to come separately in case it might be resented (vii.298–307). Finally, when Odysseus is waiting for the promised convoy home, Nausicaa contrives to be in his way for a last word, saying,

Farewell, stranger, and in your homeland remember me; it is to me first that you owe your life. (viii.459)

Odysseus makes a gallant reply, and they part. In this whole episode of Nausicaa the atmosphere is of great delicacy and tact, with transparent social fictions and hints, and its charm lies precisely in that lack of explicitness. The reader fills in what lies unspoken behind Nausicaa's last words. Dreaming about marriage, meeting a glamorous stranger, she was ready to fall in love, had not events taken a different turn.

The same sort of interest in the inscrutable hearts of women can be seen equally in the scenes with Helen, in books four and fifteen: the beautiful woman of a certain age, with a sensational past, coolly in control of things in Sparta, upstaging her amiable husband at every turn, and putting a drug in the wine to make the company forget its sorrows. Penelope, too, is always opaque, and as for Athena, Odysseus complains when she caresses him and says that she cannot leave him because he is so cunning, inventive, and self-controlled, that 'It is hard for a man to recognise you, goddess, for you transform yourself into every shape' (xiii.312–13).

Aristotle said that the plot of the *Iliad* 'is simple and a story of suffering, that of the *Odyssey* complex and a story of character' (*Poetics*, chapter 24), and it is clear that the interest in character and interest in women are intimately connected. The women of the *Odyssey* are conceived as being interesting in themselves, as being interesting because they are mysterious, and as forming a set which contrast with each other and enhance each other. This aspect of the poem was also to begin a long and important tradition. Euripides took up the interest in the feminine soul and gave it the place of honour in many of his tragedies, and following him Apollonius of Rhodes and Virgil in his *Aeneid* made the sufferings of love into a central epic theme. The tragic Dido of Virgil haunted the imagination of medieval Europe, even of great saints like Augustine for all his resistance, and helped to make tragic love into the supreme subject of so much European poetry. As so often with the *Odyssey*, we should look for the modern representatives of this tradition to the novel.

The elements of the poem which we have been discussing, the interest in detailed psychology and in the nuances of social behaviour, are not obviously heroic, and one ancient critic went so far as to call the *Odyssey* 'a sort of comedy of manners'. It certainly approaches closer to realism than the *Iliad* does. It is less paradoxical than it may appear that this realism is combined with something of a taste for magic and marvels; our own age, intolerant of the heroic in contemporary works and explicitly demanding naturalism without the false trappings of the grand manner, combines that preference with a hunger for science fiction, astrology, and magic.

Another new thing in the *Odyssey*, by contrast with the *Iliad*, is also one which is not absent in the literature of our own time: sentimentality. We have remarked on the objectivity which is a striking feature of the style of the *Iliad*, and on the conception of heroism which motivates the heroes. In the *Odyssey* the eyes of the characters are constantly going back to the past and its sufferings, and there is a tendency to shed enjoyable tears, even at moments rather to revel in grief. The attitude of the *Iliad* was the practical one of real soldiers, expressed for instance by Odysseus when he says 'We must bury those who die, steeling our hearts, mourning them for one day' (19.228), or else the violent passion of grief felt by Achilles for Patroclus or by Priam for Hector. In the *Odyssey* we find Menelaus, rich and peaceful in Sparta, leading all present in tears for the dead of the Trojan War:

So he spoke, and awoke in them all the desire to weep. Argive Helen wept, the daughter of Zeus, and Telemachus wept, and Menelaus, Atreus' son; nor was Pisistratus dry-eyed, remembering his brother Antilochus, who was slain by Memnon ... (iv.183–8)

After a time Menelaus says 'Now let us cease our weeping and think again of the feast': they all eat their fill, then Helen puts a cheering drug in the wine and tells them a story about Odysseus. We see that these tears are not deep like those of the *Iliad*, but easily aroused and easily checked again. The same rather soft sensibility is to be found in other scenes, too. Thus, when the bow of Odysseus is brought out, after twenty years, to serve as the test to select a new husband for Penelope, she goes herself to fetch it; taking it down from the hook 'she sat down and set it on her knees and wept, taking out the bow of her lord. Now when she had taken her fill of tears and lamentation, she came back to the hall' (xxi. 53–8), where the loyal retainers, too, weep at the sight of their master's bow. The scene is touching, but sentimentality is not far away.

Another device which pervades much of the poem is dramatic irony. As so many of the characters are in disguise or incognito, there are many moments at which other characters act and speak in ignorance of their real identity or of important facts known to the audience. In the first book Athena comes to Telemachus, disguised as an old friend of his father, and encourages him to feel new hope that his father will return, and to assert himself against the suitors. Telemachus, for the first time, tells them to get out of his house; there is a startled silence, and one of their leaders replies 'Telemachus, the gods themselves must be teaching you to be haughty in language and to speak boldly ...' (i.384). The point is, of course, that un-known to him this is literally true. Again, the goddess herself accompanies Telemachus on his journey to the court of Nestor at Pylos. When they arrive, they find Nestor and his household on the shore, performing a sacrifice to Poseidon, god of the sea. Telemachus is told by Athena that he must approach him and speak to him, but the bashfulness of a very young man makes him reluctant:

'How am I to go, and how shall I greet him? I am as yet unpractised in pregnant speech, and a young man feels modesty at questioning an elder.' The grey-eyed goddess Athene made answer, 'Telemachus, some things you will think of in your own mind, others a god will suggest; for I think you were not born and bred without the gods.' (iii.22–8)

The courteous son of Nestor, taking them for ordinary travel-lers, invites them to take part in the ritual, asking Athena, who seems to be the older man, to utter a prayer. Athena is delighted with him, and she prays to Poseidon; the poet concludes, 'that was her prayer, and she herself fulfilled it all' (iii.14–63). It is Athena who has always been interested in Telemachus and who will now put into his mind the words he cannot find, and her participation in an act of religious worship has a different meaning to the reader, who knows that she is herself a goddess, from the quite ordinary appearance which it wears for the characters. The long episodes in which Odysseus moves among the Phaeacians and in his own house are full of such moments, in which it is evident that the poet took particular pleasure.

The subsequent history of irony as a device and an attitude is a vast subject, but the sort which characterises the *Odyssey* is closely akin both to the tragic irony of a play like *Oedipus the King*, in which everything which happens has in reality another and a dreadful meaning from that which the hero had seen in it, and also to the comic irony of many plays of Shake-speare. The roles of Portia in the *Merchant of Venice* and of the Duke in *Measure for Measure*, for instance, make use of this kind of irony, and when the disguised Odysseus asks Eumaeus and Philoetius how they would behave if Odysseus were there (xxi.193), we approach the spirit of Shakespearean scenes in which, for instance, a girl disguised as a boy offers advice to her lover on the way to win his beloved (Rosalind in *As You Like It*).

We have said that *Iliad* is the poem of death. It is part of its whole presentation of death and life that details are avoided of the posthumous fate of the soul: we hear only that it departs lamenting from the light of this world into darkness and sense-lessness, in the mouldering realm of Hades, from which it may not return. It is the *Odyssey*, far less seriously concerned with the subject of death, which includes a full and explicit account of a visit to the world of the dead. Instead of going under the earth, Odysseus is instructed to sail to the stream of Ocean, imagined as surrounding the whole world, to a sinister wood belonging to Persephone, the queen of the dead. There the river of fire and the river of lamentation, Pyriphlegethon and Cocytus, flow together into Acheron, the river of grief, and there he is to call up the dead from Hades, sacrificing a black ewe and ram, whose blood will attract them. With the exception of the great prophet Tiresias, who alone retains the power of mind, the dead will not be able to speak unless they are allowed to drink of the blood. This of course comes from the ancient belief that the blood of a living creature is its life; the dead can regain some of the powers of life only by being given fresh blood.

What strikes the reader about this episode of the *Odyssey* is, perhaps, its avoidance of the spooky and the grisly. Even Virgil, who modelled himself on Homer, includes in his account of Aeneas' visit to the Underworld the grim figure of Charon the ferryman whose eyes are flames, and a variety of monsters; and later Latin accounts of the Underworld became more and more horrific. The poet of the *Odyssey* is still close enough to the spirit of the *Iliad*, with its determination to remove supernatural horrors from the world, to be chary of such terrors. The episodes which make an impression on the reader are those of the hero's meeting with the ghost of his mother, who tells him in simple and moving language that she died because she missed him, and his encounter with the heroes who fell at Troy, his friends. King Agamemnon tells the pitiful story of his murder by his wife and her lover: 'Indeed I had thought that I should be welcome to my wife and my household when I came home ...' (xi.430). The encounter with the shade of Achilles is also powerful. Odysseus hails him as one who was honoured like a god while he lived, and who now is a prince among the dead. Achilles is not comforted:

Try not to console me for death, shining Odysseus. Rather would I be the hired workman of another man on earth, a landless man who has but little livelihood, than be king over all the dead and departed. (xi.488)

The passage is interesting – not least because it shows, what emerges in many other places in the poem, that the position of a slave might be preferable to that of an impoverished free man – but the Achilles of the *Iliad* is greatly changed. The hero who accepted death without flinching as the price of heroism is different from the man who utters this moving but unheroic lament. Nor does the idea that dead chieftains become chieftains again in the next world find expression in the *Iliad*: it tends to soften the stark horror of death, and it would be out of place in the sterner epic. The *Odyssey* has flinched from that austere conception, which made Achilles and Thersites equal in the grave.

Finally we accompany Odysseus on what seems to be a journey through Hades, observing the posthumous punishments of certain celebrated sinners of mythology. These men – Tantalus, Sisyphus, Tityus – were guilty of personal offences against deities, they are not ordinary sinful men; we have not here, substituted for the normal Homeric picture, an afterlife with rewards and punishments for all, like that of Christian doctrine. But since they are fixed to the spot of their punishment, it is clear that what began as Odysseus standing at the edge of the Underworld and calling up the dead, has now turned into the quite different conception of the hero in the Underworld and walking about among the dead.

It is natural to suppose that a description of the next world must have serious theological implications. We know that among the Egyptians, for example, detailed accounts of the other world and instructions for one's behaviour after death were of the highest importance; at least from 400 BC, and probably earlier, Greeks in Sicily and Italy might be buried with such descriptions and instructions written on thin tablets of gold, to assist the soul on its momentous journey. In later Europe, the descent of Aeneas in the sixth book of the *Aeneid* has great moral and theological power, not to mention the *Divine Comedy* of Dante. But the eleventh book of the *Odyssey* is pure literature. As the world is dominated by heroes, so too among the dead it is heroes and heroines who monopolise the poet's attention; and the successful effects are those of pathos and nostalgia, here as in many other places in the poem. Only at the very end, when the hero is to sail away to his next adventure,

the countless tribes of the dead flocked up at me with a terrific cry. Fear seized me and turned me pale, lest dread Persephone should be sending me the head of the Gorgon, that dread monster, out of Hades. Forthwith I went to the ship and told my men to embark . . (xi.632–7)

It is an extraordinary thing to find in such an early poem an account of the world of the dead which is so little uncanny. It is almost as if the 'tribes of the dead' were simply tribes like the others which surrounded the Aegean Sea, interesting in very nearly the same way. Even the alarm which grips Odysseus at the end is barely different from that which he feels as he sails away from the Laestrygonians or the Cyclops (x.126–30). Later literature has few comparable examples of coolness on such a subject, which implies considerable sophistication both in the poet and in his audience.

Conclusion

The Homeric poems are very ancient, their manner has no real parallel in English literature, and their subject-matter may seem distant and small. Marcel Proust wrote,

The people of bygone ages seem to us infinitely remote. We are amazed when we come upon a sentiment more or less akin to what we are feeling today in a Homeric hero ... It would seem that we regarded the epic poet as being as remote from ourselves as an animal seen in a zoo. (*The Guermantes Way*, tr. Scott Moncrieff, ii.150)

The argument of this book has been that the epics are in fact highly sophisticated productions, which are by no means simply archaic and semi-savage tales of adventure but convey ideas of lasting depth and importance; nor are they so removed from us in time and place as to be unintelligible.

The poet of the *Iliad* used traditional material and forms to create a new work, which embodies a radical and consistent interpretation of the world and of the position of man. As far as possible everything is cleared away which could distract attention from the terrible contrast of life and death. The hero represents the summit of human greatness, and his struggle to face death is fascinating enough to attract the gaze of the immortal gods and so to exalt human life to a level at which it achieves significance and becomes a fit subject for the song which celebrates its fragility and its greatness.

The *Odyssey*, less intense, more inclusive, with its wide range of interest in the world and all its variety, has a different conception of the gods and of heroism. Gods and heroes alike need and receive moral justification, of a sort much closer to our ideas. Odysseus, the hero of endurance and guile, replaces Achilles, the hero of openness and dash, in a world grown full of treachery, deception, and complexity; and he must contend with disloyal subordinates and exotic monsters. We find a different kind of realism, and also a sort of escapism.

The Homeric poems do not tell us that the world was made for man, or that our natural state in it is one of happiness. They do say that it can be comprehended in human terms, and that human life can be more than an insignificant or ignoble struggle in the dark. The human soul can rise to the height of the challenges and the suffering which are the lot of all mankind. That spirit, chastened but not despairing, which sees the world without illusion and confronts it without self-pity or evasion, was the gift of Greece to the world, and it is the deepest element in the thought of Homer.

Translations and texts

There have been many translations of Homer into English. The famous version by Alexander Pope was dismissed by the great scholar Richard Bentley ('It is a pretty poem, Mr Pope, but you must not call it Homer'), but praised by Samuel Johnson ('A performance which no age or nation can pretend to equal'). It has great liveliness and poetic power, but it is at times a long way from the less rhetorical and less pointed spirit of the original.

In 1865 the Earl of Derby produced a very competent rendering into blank verse. The translations in this book have made use of two late Victorian versions; of the *Iliad* by Lang, Leaf, and Myers, and of the *Odyssey* by Butcher and Lang. They aim at a dignified and rather archaic prose. T. E. Lawrence produced a rather mannered version of the *Odyssey* in 1932, under the name of T. E. Shaw; he took a surprisingly low view of the original. The Penguin Classic translations by E. V. Rieu (*Odyssey*, 1946; *Iliad*, 1951) turn the poems into a very readable but unpoetical modern prose idiom. W. Shewring has produced a prose version of the *Odyssey* (Oxford, 1980) which is more ambitious stylistically, with an interesting discussion of the problems of translating Homer. Professor R. Lattimore has translated both epics into modern verse (*Iliad*, Chicago, 1951; *Odyssey*, New York, 1967).

For the Greek text the Oxford Classical Text by T. W. Allen and D. B. Monro is as good as any; there is also a Loeb Library edition with facing English translation by A. T. Murray.

Further reading

Arnold, Matthew. *On Translating Homer*, London, 1862; often reprinted. A great poet discusses the style of Homer and criticises some attempts at translation.

Edwards, Mark W. *Homer: Poet of the Iliad*, Johns Hopkins, 1987. Systematic treatment, with bibliography, of the central aspects of the poem.

C. Emlyn-Jones, L. Hardwick, and J. Purkis (editors): *Homer: Readings and Images*, Duckworth and Open University, 1992. A good collection of essays by various scholars.

Finley, Sir Moses. *The World of Odysseus*, second edition, London, 1977. A readable account of the sociology of the *Odyssey*.

Fränkel, H. *Early Greek Poetry and Philosophy*, translated by Hadas and Willis, Oxford, 1975. The section on Homer contains many interesting insights.

Griffin, J. *Homer on Life and Death*, Oxford, 1980. Brings out the uniqueness of the Homeric treatment of central aspects of human life.

Griffin, J. *Homer: The Odyssey*. Cambridge (Landmarks of World Literature series), 1987. Concise critical introduction to the poem.

Kirk, G. S. *The Songs of Homer*, Cambridge, 1962. A full discussion of the poems from the point of view of oral poetry.

Lloyd-Jones, H. *The Justice of Zeus*, Berkeley, 1971. Homeric ideas about the justice of the gods are put in the context of later Greek developments.

Murray, G. *The Rise of the Greek Epic*, fourth edition, Oxford, 1934. Imaginative and lively account of the creation of the poems and their setting.

Otto, W. F. *The Homeric Gods*, translated by Hadas, London, 1954. Exciting (if rather one-sidedly 'Apollonian') account of the gods as conceived in early Greece.

Silk, M. *Homer: The Iliad*. Cambridge (Landmarks of World Literature series), 1987. Concise critical introduction to the poem.

Weil, Simone. 'The Iliad, Poem of Might' in *Intimations of Christianity Among the Ancient Greeks*, edited and translated by E. C. Geissbuhler, London, 1957. A brilliantly suggestive essay on the *Iliad* and its picture of human suffering.

Index

OXFORD

MORE OXFORD PAPERBACKS

This book is just one of nearly 1000 Oxford Paperbacks currently in print. If you would like details of other Oxford Paperbacks, including titles in the World's Classics, Oxford Reference, Oxford Books, OPUS, Past Masters, Oxford Authors, and Oxford Shakespeare series, please write to:

UK and Europe: Oxford Paperbacks Publicity Manager, Arts and Reference Publicity Department, Oxford University Press, Walton Street, Oxford OX2 6DP.

Customers in UK and Europe will find Oxford Paperbacks available in all good bookshops. But in case of difficulty please send orders to the Cash-with-Order Department, Oxford University Press Distribution Services, Saxon Way West, Corby, Northants NN18 9ES. Tel: 01536 741519; Fax: 01536 746337. Please send a cheque for the total cost of the books, plus £1.75 postage and packing for orders under £20; £2.75 for orders over £20. Customers outside the UK should add 10% of the cost of the books for postage and packing.

USA: Oxford Paperbacks Marketing Manager, Oxford University Press, Inc., 200 Madison Avenue, New York, N.Y. 10016.

Canada: Trade Department, Oxford University Press, 70 Wynford Drive, Don Mills, Ontario M3C 1J9.

Australia: Trade Marketing Manager, Oxford University Press, G.P.O. Box 2784Y, Melbourne 3001, Victoria.

South Africa: Oxford University Press, P.O. Box 1141, Cape Town 8000.

PAST
MASTERS

PAST MASTERS

A wide range of unique, short, clear introductions to the lives and work of the world's most influential thinkers. Written by experts, they cover the history of ideas from Aristotle to Wittgenstein. Readers need no previous knowledge of the subject, so they are ideal for students and general readers alike.

Each book takes as its main focus the thought and work of its subject. There is a short section on the life and a final chapter on the legacy and influence of the thinker. A section of further reading helps in further research.

The series continues to grow, and future Past Masters will include **Owen Gingerich** on *Copernicus*, **R G Frey** on *Joseph Butler*, **Bhiku Parekh** on *Gandhi*, **Christopher Taylor** on *Socrates*, **Michael Inwood** on *Heidegger*, and **Peter Ghosh** on *Weber*.

PAST MASTERS

KEYNES

Robert Skidelsky

John Maynard Keynes is a central thinker of the twentieth century. This is the only available short introduction to his life and work.

Keynes's doctrines continue to inspire strong feelings in admirers and detractors alike. This short, engaging study of his life and thought explores the many positive and negative stereotypes and also examines the quality of Keynes's mind, his cultural and social milieu, his ethical and practical philosophy, and his monetary thought. Recent scholarship has significantly altered the treatment and assessment of Keynes's contribution to twentieth-century economic thinking, and the current state of the debate initiated by the Keynesian revolution is discussed in a final chapter on its legacy.

MASTERS

RUSSELL

A. C. Grayling

Bertrand Russell (1872–1970) is one of the most famous and important philosophers of the twentieth century. In this account of his life and work A. C. Grayling introduces both his technical contributions to logic and philosophy, and his wide-ranging views on education, politics, war, and sexual morality. Russell is credited with being one of the prime movers of Analytic Philosophy, and with having played a part in the revolution in social attitudes witnessed throughout the twentieth-century world. This introduction gives a clear survey of Russell's achievements across their whole range.

OXFORD

RETHINKING LIFE AND DEATH
THE COLLAPSE OF OUR TRADITIONAL ETHICS

Peter Singer

A victim of the Hillsborough Disaster in 1989, Anthony Bland lay in hospital in a coma being fed liquid food by a pump, via a tube passing through his nose and into his stomach. On 4 February 1993 Britain's highest court ruled that doctors attending him could lawfully act to end his life.

Our traditional ways of thinking about life and death are collapsing. In a world of respirators and embryos stored for years in liquid nitrogen, we can no longer take the sanctity of human life as the cornerstone of our ethical outlook.

In this controversial book Peter Singer argues that we cannot deal with the crucial issues of death, abortion, euthanasia and the rights of nonhuman animals unless we sweep away the old ethic and build something new in its place.

Singer outlines a new set of commandments, based on compassion and commonsense, for the decisions everyone must make about life and death.

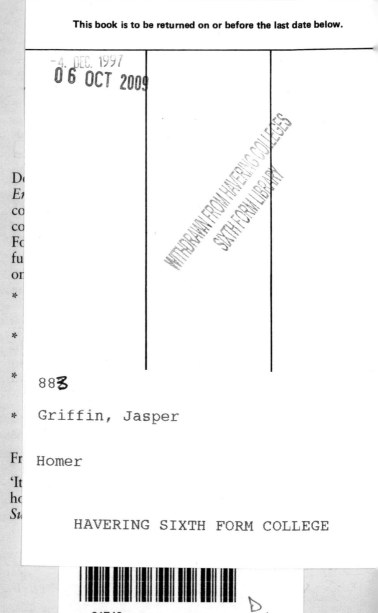